CONTENTS

INTRODUCTION

Rationale

Current literature on teaching reading reveals that using trade books in the classroom is gaining in popularity. For example, Bernice E. Cullinan (1987), former International Reading Association president, has written and spoken about the power of trade books to overcome "aliteracy," a term used for those who can read but don't read and/or won't read. William Bennett, former U.S. Secretary of Education, recommended using more trade books in the elementary classroom as a way to overcome "the dreadening quality of what children are given to read." Bill Honig (1986), State Superintendent of Public Education, implemented the California Reading Initiative Program, which consists of curriculum guidebooks to accompany the use of over 1,000 recommended trade books for the classroom. The use of trade books in an attempt to overcome illiteracy in the United States is mounting. Most recently, First Lady Barbara Bush announced the formation of the Barbara Bush Foundation for Family Literacy, which will give grants to programs that focus on the family as the key to a more literate nation.

One primary motivation for integrating trade books into the curriculum is research showing convincingly that reading to and with children works best (Doake, 1979; Durkin, 1966; Holdaway, 1979; IRA, 1986a, 1986b; Schickedanz, 1983, 1986). In addition to learning to read, children develop personal preferences and special interests in books through this early exposure to literature and are thereby motivated to pursue books of their own choice. Proponents of literature-based reading programs agree that their success should be measured in terms of the number of students who eventually establish the habit of reading for independent learning, personal pleasure, and continued growth.

The attitudes children develop toward reading are also of great importance. As Bruno Bettelheim (1981) so poignantly stated, "A child's attitude toward reading is of such importance that, more often than not, it determines his scholastic fate. Moreover, his experience in learning to read may decide how he will feel about learning in general, and even about himself as a person." Ulrich Hardt (1983) has supported this view: "Children will become readers only if their emotions have been engaged, their imaginations stirred and stretched by what they find on printed pages. One sure way to make this happen is through literature."

Integrating literature into the curriculum does not mean that teachers need to abandon the basal reader. Trade books can be used to supplement and enhance the basal reader program. Cullinan (1987) has reported that even though 85 to 90 percent of the elementary classrooms across the United States use the basal reading series as the core instructional resource, no basal series was ever intended to be a complete, self-contained reading program. Therefore, it is important that teachers learn methods and techniques for integrating literature into the curriculum, as well as acquire materials for doing so.

Many publishers are responding by publishing guidebooks, kits, and workbooks to aid teachers. *Read It Again! Book 2*, the second in a series of guidebooks written by Liz Rothlein and Terri Christman, provides instructors with imaginative teaching ideas to use with fifteen easily accessible, popular,

READ IT AGAIN!

Book 2
A Guide for Teaching Reading Through Literature

Liz Rothlein
Terri Christman

Illustrated by Sue Breitner

SCOTT, FORESMAN AND COMPANY
GLENVIEW, ILLINOIS   LONDON

To Mom and Dad, with love.—L.R.

I am dedicating this book to my parents. Thanks for making so many things possible for me. Together, you encouraged and supported me in becoming who I am. Today, tomorrow, and forever you are in my heart and thoughts.—T.C.

Acknowledgments

To Thomas L., who through the years shared his happiness and gave me continued support. I am sending you a warm and sincere thanks.—T.C.

To Ashman for spelling any word for me any time. Thanks for sharing your talents.—T.C.

Many thanks to Anita Meinbach, whose careful review and constructive criticism lent polish and substance to our final draft.—L.R. & T.C.

Good Year Books
are available for preschool through grade 8 and for every basic curriculum subject plus many enrichment areas. For more Good Year Books, contact your local bookseller or educational dealer. For a complete catalog with information about other Good Year Books, please write:

> **Good Year Books**
> Department GYB
> 1900 East Lake Avenue
> Glenview, Illinois 60025

quality children's books. Students in grades three through five will benefit from the materials as they develop a love for reading and thinking. The activity sheets emphasize the interactive processes of speaking, listening, reading, and writing. Activities are included that involve the children in music, art, process writing, cooking, geography, and poetry. The discussion questions suggested for each book reflect B. S. Bloom's (1956) taxonomy and focus on developing higher-order thinking skills, requiring students to analyze, synthesize, and evaluate.

Read It Again! Book 2 can be adapted to almost any classroom setting. It will be particularly beneficial to resource room teachers, teachers in gifted programs, and librarians. The activities can be presented to large or small groups, are designed for different levels of ability, and can be used to encourage independent work.

Read It Again! Book 2 is also an excellent resource for parents. The suggested books and activities will help parents develop in their children an appreciation for literature and reading, as well as the skills necessary to become effective and involved readers.

Objectives

Read It Again! Book 2 is designed to enable students to develop vital thinking and learning skills. The activities will help students meet the following objectives, developed by the National Council of Teachers of English (1983):

1. Realize the importance of literature as a mirror of human experience, reflecting human motives, conflicts, and values
2. Be able to identify with fictional characters in human situations as a means of relating to others; gain insights from involvement with literature
3. Become aware of important writers representing diverse backgrounds and traditions in literature
4. Become familiar with masterpieces of literature, both past and present
5. Develop effective ways of talking and writing about varied forms of literature
6. Experience literature as a way to appreciate the rhythms and beauty of the language
7. Develop habits of reading that carry over into adult life

Features

Read It Again! Book 2 focuses on the following fifteen easy-to-find books, which are listed by suggested reading level. These books have a proven track record of success with children. Many of them are Newbery Award winners.

Third Grade Reading Level
Chocolate Fever, by Robert Kimmel Smith
The Giving Tree, by Shel Silverstein
The Reluctant Dragon, by Kenneth Grahame
Sarah, Plain and Tall, by Patricia MacLachlan
The Whipping Boy, by Sid Fleischman

Fourth Grade Reading Level
Bridge to Terabithia, by Katherine Paterson
Charlotte's Web, by E. B. White
The Hundred Dresses, by Eleanor Estes
James and the Giant Peach, by Roald Dahl
Ramona the Pest, by Beverly Cleary

Fifth Grade Reading Level
Call It Courage, by Armstrong Sperry
The Lion, the Witch, and the Wardrobe, by C. S. Lewis
The Little House in the Big Woods, by Laura Ingalls Wilder
The Secret Garden, by Frances Hodgson Burnett
Sounder, by William H. Armstrong

Note: Although the books are listed by reading level, the interest level of the books spans grade three through grade seven.

The following basic information is provided for each book: author, illustrator, publisher, publication date, number of pages, appropriate reading and interest levels, other works by the same author, and information about the author.

Next comes a summary of the book and an introduction to use when presenting the book to children. Key vocabulary words from the stories are then listed.

Next are discussion questions, designed to foster higher-level thinking skills. Finally, bulletin board ideas are offered as reinforcement activities. Many of these activities require class participation with minimal teacher direction.

The major feature of the book is the reproducible activity sheets provided for each selection. These activity sheets can easily be correlated with basic objectives in language arts and literature, as well as the social sciences. For flexibility and ease of use, the activity sheets have been numbered according to level of difficulty. Activity Sheet 1 is designed to be the easiest, and Activity Sheet 3 is designed to be the most difficult. However, all three activity sheets may be used by one student: Activity Sheet 1 could be considered an independent activity, Activity Sheet 2 an instructional activity, and Activity Sheet 3 an enrichment activity. Teachers and parents can determine which activities are most appropriate to meet each child's individual needs.

In addition to the reproducible activity sheets, optional ideas for activities are also provided. These include activities for group or individual participation.

The appendix contains general activity sheets that can be used after all the selected books in *Read It Again! Book 2* have been read. These activities can be reproduced or can be adhered to tagboard and laminated, then used for independent learning center activities. Also in the appendix is a selection of book report forms, directions for how to make a book, and a list of all the vocabulary words introduced for the selected books. This list of words can be used to create additional reinforcement activities for the students. Finally, an answer key to activities is provided for teachers' and parents' convenience.

Guidelines for Developing Book Units

Teachers may find that some of their students' favorite books are not available in guidebooks like *Read It Again!* and *Read It Again! Book 2*. By following some simple guidelines, teachers can develop their own "book units" based on books of their choice:

1. Select the book, taking the following into consideration:
   a. Use books that are well written. Children especially enjoy stories with a strong, fast-paced plot and memorable, interesting, well-delineated characters they can identify with.
   b. Select books that reflect students' interests. Use interest inventories

and talk with your students about what they like. Books are more appealing when they relate to specific interests or when students can identify with the characters, learning how others deal with situations and problems similar to their own experiences.

   c. Select books that will stimulate their imaginations.

   d. Select books from a variety of genres. Books of fiction (realistic fiction, historical fiction, fantasy, folklore) provide students with characters and emotions they can identify with and establish settings and themes that captivate their imaginations and explore the human condition. Poetry should be included too. Nonfiction books (informational books and biographies) arm students with the facts and background they'll need to connect new concepts and knowledge.

   e. Select books that represent both traditional and modern literature. Modern literature reflects contemporary settings, themes, language, and characters. Traditional literature provides links with the past and carries readers to another place and time.

   f. Select several books by the same author to help students gain an appreciation for the style and works of authors of outstanding children's literature.

   g. Select books that cover a specific theme or concept currently being developed in class.

2. Once the book has been selected, develop the unit using the following topics:

   a. Title of book

   b. Name of author and illustrator

   c. Publisher and date of publication

   d. Number of pages

   e. Reading level

   f. Interest level

   g. Other books by the author

   h. Information about the author: This information can be found in *Something About the Author: Facts and Pictures About Authors and Illustrators of Books for Young Children* and *Yesterday's Authors for Children.*

   i. Summary of the book: The summary helps teachers remember what the book is about. It also helps students decide if they want to read the book. The summary should identify the main characters and concisely reveal the plot.

   j. Introduction to the book: The introduction needs to present a purpose and/or motivation for reading the book. The introduction often includes a statement that relates to the readers or asks a question that can be answered once the text has been read.

   k. Key vocabulary words: Select and define some of the words that students may not be familiar with and that are important to understanding the story.

   l. Discussion questions: Asking good questions is one of the most vital aspects of developing comprehension and thinking skills. Good questions:

     • Are relevant: Asking too many questions interferes with students' enjoyment of the story. Questions that simply require students to answer with facts stated in the text do little to enhance comprehension and higher-order thinking. Ask questions that are meaningful.

• Foster higher-level thinking: It is vital that questions be written at different levels. Although literal questions (knowledge and comprehension) are important to ascertain students' understanding of the story, questions should be included that ask students to analyze ("the reason that," "what are the causes," "what are the consequences," "examine evidence"), synthesize ("create," "devise," "design,"), and evaluate ("what is good/bad," "what do you like best," "judge the evidence"). These higher-order questions are especially important for fostering critical and creative thinking.

• Help students reach an understanding of an issue or concept: Questions should flow and reflect a sense of continuity rather than be isolated. In this way, students will be guided to form their own conclusions and judgments.

• Encourage application of background knowledge, ideas, and experiences.

After asking a question, students should be given time to reflect on possible responses. A wait of 3 to 5 seconds is generally recommended. Often it will be necessary to rephrase a question to reach students' level of understanding.

   m. Bulletin Board: Create a bulletin board that relates to the book, and give students a chance to participate in constructing it.

   n. Activity sheets: Construct activity sheets that relate to some aspect of the book as well as the competencies being taught in the curriculum. For example, if students are working on letter writing, after reading *Charlotte's Web*, have them write a letter to Mr. Arable telling him why he should not kill Wilbur.

   o. Additional activities: Create an ongoing list of activities that relate to the book. These may include art, drama, movement, cooking, science, and social studies.

3. Develop an organizational system for storing and filing the book units, such as file folders, small boxes, or manila envelopes. The book, bulletin board letters, and other related materials can then be kept from year to year. Eventually, teachers will have a collection of book units.

Guidelines for Using the Book

Before using the activities in *Read It Again! Book 2*, it is important that the teacher or parent present the selected books in an interesting and meaningful way. Students should enjoy themselves as well as develop skills that will benefit them as they read on their own. One way of presenting the books is through reading aloud. The following suggestions may be helpful:

1. Establish a regular schedule for reading aloud.
2. Practice reading the book to acquaint yourself with the story's concepts in advance.
3. Have a prereading session to set the stage. Include the title of the book, the author's and illustrator's names, an introduction or purpose for listening to the story, an introduction of key vocabulary words, and a discussion about the main parts of the book, such as the book jacket, end pages, author information, and so on.
4. Create a comfortable atmosphere in which distractions are minimal.
5. Read with feeling and expression. Careful attention to vocal pitch and stress is necessary if spoken dialogue is to sound like conversation.

6. When appropriate, hold the book so everyone can see the print and the illustrations.
7. Allow the children to participate in the story when appropriate. Occasionally, you may want to stop and ask students what they think might happen next or how the story may end.
8. Provide opportunities to respond to the story. Although it is not necessary for students to respond to every story, they can benefit from such follow-up activities as discussion questions, dramatizations, art activities, book reports, and so on.

Another way of presenting books to students is through a silent reading period, often referred to as sustained silent reading (SSR). SSR provides students with an opportunity to read independently. The following suggestions may be helpful in setting up an SSR program in your classroom:
1. Provide students with a wide selection of books to choose from.
2. Allow time for students to browse through the books and select one to read.
3. Provide a regular time each day for SSR, so students come to expect this period as a permanent part of their routine.
4. Start the program with 5 to 10 minutes, depending on students' reading abilities, then gradually increase the time.
5. Make sure everyone reads, including the teacher.
6. Allow a time at the end of SSR for students to share what they have read. Ask questions, such as "What is something interesting you read about today?" "What characters did you like best?" "Why?"

The flexible format of *Read It Again! Book 2* allows the teacher or parent to use it in a variety of ways. The books and many of the activities can be presented in any order, although the following format is suggested:
1. Introduce the selected book.
2. Introduce the vocabulary words.
3. Read the book aloud, or provide individual copies of the book and time for the students to read it themselves.
4. Ask the discussion questions.
5. Put up the bulletin board.
6. Introduce the activity sheet(s).
7. Do appropriate additional activities.
8. Provide appropriate general activities.

The amount of time allotted to each book will depend on several factors, including age and grade level of the students and flexibility of time and scheduling. What is important is to have fun and get students addicted to books!

References

Bennett, William J. *First Lessons: A Report on Elementary Education in America.* Washington, D.C.: U.S. Government Printing Office, 1986.

Bettelheim, Bruno. "Attitudes Toward Reading." *Atlantic Monthly,* Nov. 1981, p. 25.

Bloom, B. S., M. B. Englehart, S. J. Furst, W. H. Hill, and D. R. Krathwohl. *Taxonomy of Educational Objectives. The Classification of Educational Goals. Handbook I: Cognitive Domain.* New York: Longmans Green, 1956.

Cullinan, Bernice E. "Books in the Classroom." *The Horn Book,* Nov./Dec. 1986, Vol. 62, pp. 766–768.

Cullinan, Bernice E. (ed.). *Children's Literature in the Reading Program.* Newark, Del.: International Reading Association, 1987.

Doake, David. "Book Experience and Emergent Reading Behavior." Paper presented at Preconvention Institute No. 24, Research on Written Language Development, International Reading Association annual convention, Atlanta, April 1979.

Durkin, Dolores. *Children Who Read Early.* New York: Teachers' College Press, 1966.

Hardt, Ulrich. *Teaching Reading with the Other Language Arts.* Newark, Del.: International Reading Association, 1983, p. 108.

Holdaway, Don. *The Foundations of Literacy.* Toronto: Ashton Scholastic, 1979.

International Reading Association. "IRA Position Statement on Reading and Writing in Early Childhood." *The Reading Teacher*, Oct. 1986, Vol. 39, pp. 822–824.

International Reading Association. "Literacy Development and Pre-First Grade: A Joint Statement of Concerns About Present Practices in Pre-First Grade Reading Instruction and Recommendation for Improvement." *Young Children*, Nov. 1986, Vol. 41, pp. 10–13.

National Council of English Teachers, "Essentials of English." *Language Arts*, Feb. 1983, Vol. 60, pp. 244–248.

Schickedanz, J. *Helping Children Learn About Reading.* Washington, D.C.: NAEYC, 1983.

Schickedanz, J. *More Than the ABCs: The Early Stages of Reading and Writing.* Washington, D.C.: NAEYC, 1986.

SELECTED BOOKS AND ACTIVITIES

CHOCOLATE FEVER

Author
Robert Kimmel Smith

Illustrator
Gioia Fiammenghi

Publisher
Dell Publishing, 1972

Pages 93	Reading Level 3	Interest Level 3–5

Other Books by Smith
Jelly Belly; The War with Grandpa

Information About the Author
Robert Kimmel Smith was born on July 31, 1930, in Brooklyn, New York, where he continues to live. He is married and has two children. He has been a full-time writer since 1970. He has written many plays and novels; however, he is currently concentrating mostly on writing plays, films, and television scripts, with an occasional novel. He said he learned to write when he was in the advertising business and wrote advertisements and commercials. Mr. Smith got the idea to write the book *Chocolate Fever* from his daughter. It came about because he told his daughter a story about a little boy who liked chocolate very much. The little boy who liked chocolate so much happened to be him, Mr. Smith! He kept telling the story over and over, and sometimes he'd forget parts. So his daughter suggested that he write it out. He did, and it became the book *Chocolate Fever.*

Summary
Henry Green is a boy in love with chocolate. He loves it so much that he eats it for breakfast, lunch, and dinner. He probably loves chocolate more than anyone else does. And chocolate seems to love him. It doesn't seem to make him fat. It doesn't seem to hurt his teeth. It doesn't stunt his growth. It doesn't hurt his skin. It doesn't seem to give him a bellyache. So Henry's parents allow him to eat as much chocolate as he likes. One day, however, he develops "chocolate fever." Then he finds himself caught up in quite an adventure.

Introduction
Henry Green loves chocolate. What is your favorite food? Could you eat it for breakfast, lunch, and dinner?

Key Vocabulary

phenomenon	prodded	earnestly	survive	cautiously
nauseating	bluffing	hijacked	cargo	desolate
acquaintance	mirth	subsided	breeds	dumbfounded

From *Read It Again: Book 2, A Guide for Teaching Reading Through Literature* published by Scott, Foresman and Company. Copyright © 1990 Liz Rothlein and Terri Christman.

CHOCOLATE FEVER

Discussion Questions

1 In the beginning of the story, the author tells us that some people say Henry Green wasn't really born but was hatched, fully grown, from a chocolate bean. Explain this. (Answers may vary.)

2 Describe a typical breakfast for Henry. (Answers may vary, but might include chocolate cake, a bowl of cocoa-crispy cereal and milk with chocolate syrup, a glass of chocolate milk, chocolate cookies, and chocolate ice cream.)

3 A lot of people in the book try to guess what Henry Green has. What are some of the guesses? (They guess that Henry fell in a mud puddle or that he has freckles, measles, chicken pox, or an unidentified rash.)

4 Why does Henry run away from the hospital? (Answers may vary but might include being tired or afraid or wanting to be left alone or at home.)

5 After running away from the hospital, Henry hides out in a garage. Describe the thoughts that go through his head at that time. (Answers may vary.)

6 How does Henry trick the boys in the schoolyard? (He tells them that if they touch him they will die.)

7 What do Henry and Mac have in common? (Both have been stared at.)

8 What lesson does Henry learn? (Answers may vary but might include the idea that we can't have everything we want everytime we want it.)

Bulletin Board

In the story, the thieves think they are hijacking a truckload of furs. Instead they are getting a truckload of candy bars. On the bulletin board, place the caption "A TRUCKLOAD OF . . ." Have students cut out the truck pattern and draw on the truck what they want inside it.

Name _____ Date _____

ACTIVITY
SHEET 1

Directions
Henry eats many unusual things—for example, chocolate-covered fried chicken, chocolate sprinkles on top of buttered noodles, cocoa on peaches, and mashed potatoes with chocolate syrup. Below, on the left, draw some of the things Henry eats. On the right, draw what you are eating today for breakfast, lunch, and dinner.

Henry	**You**
Breakfast	
Lunch	
Dinner	

CHOCOLATE FEVER

Name _____ Date _____

Directions
Listed below are many events from the story. Read each phrase, and write it under the correct description of where it takes place.

Events
a. Eating breakfast
b. Talking to Michael
c. Being laughed at by students
d. Being chased by doctors, nurses, guards, and police
e. Meeting the boys in the schoolyard
f. Riding in Mac's truck
g. Doing fractions

h. Going to the infirmary
i. Being examined by Dr. Fargo
j. Jumping off the examining table
k. Sleeping in the garage
l. Being hijacked
m. Getting ready for school
n. Trying cinnamon
o. Meeting Alfred Cane

It happens at home.	It happens at school.
_____	_____
_____	_____
_____	_____
_____	_____
_____	_____
It happens at the hospital.	**It happens while Henry is running away.**
_____	_____
_____	_____
_____	_____
_____	_____
_____	_____

Name _____ Date _____

ACTIVITY SHEET 3

Directions

Match what the character says, from the quotations at the bottom of the page, to the characters. Put the letter of the quotation in the blanks provided and then draw, in the circles, what you think the character looks like.

Henry Green

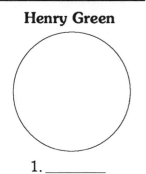

1. _____

Mr. Green

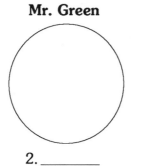

2. _____

Mrs. Green (Enid)

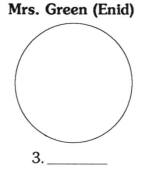

3. _____

Mark Green

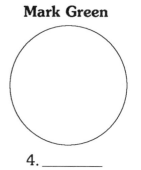

4. _____

Mrs. Kimmelfarber

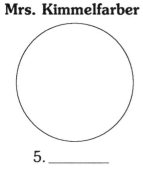

5. _____

Nurse Farthing

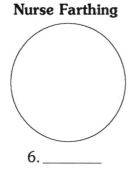

6. _____

Dr. Fargo

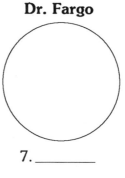

7. _____

Mac

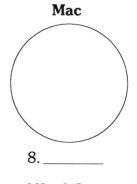

8. _____

Mrs. Macintosh

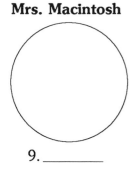

9. _____

Mr. Pangalo

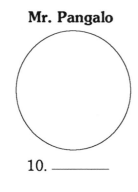

10. _____

Lefty

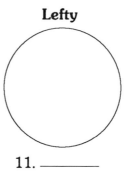

11. _____

Alfred Cane

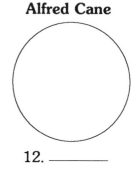

12. _____

Quotations

a. "So all that staring and stuff, what it did was make me proud."
b. "Just one more chocolate cookie."
c. "The light is always green for the Greens."
d. "How does Henry like his chocolate?"
e. "I'm right in the middle of Americus Vespucci!"
f. "Take this to the laboratory at once."
g. "Let's go, slowpoke, we don't want to be late."

h. "And if I take six and a half and subtract one and a quarter, what will I have left?"
i. "Hey, sleepyhead, are you going to sleep forever?"
j. "You said this job would be like taking candy from a baby."
k. "Dirt breeds germs, and germs have a nasty way of making healthy people ill."
l. "Although life is grand and pleasure is everywhere, we can't have everything we want everytime we want it."

From *Read It Again: Book 2, A Guide for Teaching Reading Through Literature* published by Scott, Foresman and Company. Copyright © 1990 Liz Rothlein and Terri Christman.

CHOCOLATE FEVER

From *Read It Again: Book 2, A Guide for Teaching Reading Through Literature* published by Scott, Foresman and Company. Copyright © 1990 Liz Rothlein and Terri Christman.

Additional Activities

1 In the story, Mac drives a truck full of candy bars. Have students bring in candy bar wrappers for a week. Make a collage using all the wrappers. Discuss the many types of candy bars that exist, the ingredients, students' favorites, the most common, and so on.

2 Henry makes medical history with the only case of chocolate fever. Henry suffers from chocolate fever because he eats too much chocolate. The most visible evidence of chocolate fever is big brown spots (pure chocolate) that pop out all over his body. Have students create other types of "fevers"—for example, pizza fever. Then have them describe the symptoms and illustrate how a person would look with the "fever" they create.

3 Have students help list all the characters in *Chocolate Fever* as you write their names on the chalkboard (Mr. Green, Enid Green, Mark Green, Mrs. Macintosh, Elizabeth Green, Michael Burke, Mrs. Kimmelfarber, Mr. Pangalo, Nurse Fathing, Dr. Fargo, Mac, Louie, Lefty, and Alfred Cane). Have students determine whether these people have a positive or negative relationship with Henry. Put a plus sign next to the name if that person is positive toward Henry, a minus sign if the person is negative. Then in a sentence, students can describe what each character did to make Henry feel positive or negative.

4 In Chapter 12, Daddy Green tells Henry, while he is eating breakfast, that the candy bar company is going to give him some kind of award for helping to foil the hijacking. Have students predict, orally or in writing, what Henry might possibly get as an award.

5 Chocolate is made from the seeds of the cocoa tree. Cocoa trees can be raised only near the equator. The trees are about 20 feet tall. They have long, leathery leaves and small pink blossoms. The scientific name of this tree is *Theobroma cacao.* It means "food for the gods." Many people love chocolate and would agree the name is a good one. Draw a tree on the chalkboard and label it *Cocoa Tree.* Then do a semantic mapping or webbing using the word "cocoa" by having the students think of all the things made from a cocoa tree, such as chocolate pie, chocolate chip cookies, fudge, brownies, and hot chocolate.

6 In the story, Henry's favorite food is chocolate. Tell students to survey friends, neighbors, and family members to find out what each person's favorite food is. To record their findings, students can list each person's name and, next to it, his or her favorite food. After all students have completed this assignment, find out which food was mentioned most frequently, next most frequently, and so on. Make a graph showing the number of people liking each food.

THE GIVING TREE

Author
Shel Silverstein

Publisher
Harper & Row, 1964

Pages 55	Reading Level 3	Interest Level 3–4

Other Books by Silverstein
*Where the Sidewalk Ends;
The Addict; The Missing
Piece; Lafcadio, the Lion Who
Shot Back*

Information About the Author

Shel Silverstein was born in Chicago, Illinois, in 1932. His creative books appeal to both children and grownups. He is known not only as a writer of books but also as a poet, cartoonist, composer, lyricist, and folksinger. He wrote the hit song "A Boy Named Sue," which was recorded by Johnny Cash. Mr. Silverstein never planned to write or draw for children. His book, *The Giving Tree*, was rejected at first but has since been a great success. He says this book is simply about a relationship between two people, one who gives and one who takes. He spends his time now living in Greenwich Village, in Key West, or on his houseboat in Sausalito, California.

Summary

An apple tree is very happy when a boy eats its apples, swings on its branches, and climbs up its trunk. It is sad and lonely when the boy ignores it. The tree has something to offer the boy at different stages of his life. Giving makes the tree very happy. This book takes a simple and tender look at friendship, love, and sharing.

Introduction

This story is about an apple tree and a boy. Giving makes the apple tree very happy, and receiving makes the boy happy. How do you feel when you give something to someone? Which do you prefer, to give or to receive?

Key Vocabulary

gather	shade	trunk	forest	sailed
stump	climbed	carried	branches	leaves

THE GIVING TREE

Discussion Questions

1 Name three things that the tree gives the boy when he is young. (The tree gives apples to eat, branches to swing on, a trunk to climb up.)

2 Why is the tree lonely when the boy grows up? (Answers may vary but may include the following: because the boy doesn't visit as often or because he no longer climbs up its trunk, swings from its branches, eats its apples.)

3 What two things does the boy do with the apples he gets from the tree? (He eats them and sells them.)

4 What does the boy use from the tree to make his house? (He uses the branches.)

5 What could the boy do for the tree? (Answers may vary.)

6 Do you think the boy is selfish? Why or why not? (Answers may vary.)

7 How do you think the tree would feel if the boy did not take all it offers? (Answers may vary.)

8 What part of the story could be true? (Answers may vary but could include the boy playing in the tree and eating the apples or the boy selling the apples.)
What part of the story is make-believe? (Answers may vary but could include the tree talking and feeling emotions.)

Bulletin Board

Draw a large tree trunk with branches to represent an apple tree. Place it on the bulletin board. Using large cutout letters, put the caption "THE GIVING TREE" above the tree. Duplicate the apple pattern below so each student has one. Then ask students to write, on the apple, what they could give to someone. Finally, put all the students' apples on the branches of the tree.

Name _____ Date _____

From *Read It Again: Book 2, A Guide for Teaching Reading Through Literature* published by Scott, Foresman and Company. Copyright © 1990 Liz Rothlein and Terri Christman.

**ACTIVITY
SHEET 1**

Directions
In *The Giving Tree*, the boy cuts down the tree to make a boat. Today there is much concern about the conservation of trees. Create a campaign, similar to the "Just Say No to Drugs" campaign, to aid in the conservation of trees. The following steps will help you plan and carry out your campaign.

1. List reasons for having a campaign against cutting trees.

_____

_____

_____

2. Create a slogan for the campaign, one that is clever and catchy and that will remind others about the problems of cutting trees. Use this slogan to create a button and bumper sticker for the campaign.

_____

_____

_____

_____

3. List events you and your school could sponsor and guest speakers you could invite to help your campaign against cutting trees.

_____

_____

4. List the steps you will follow to get the campaign started and to get others involved.

_____

_____

_____

THE RELUCTANT DRAGON

Author
Kenneth Grahame

Illustrator
Ernest H. Shepard

Publisher
Holiday House, 1953

Pages 54	Reading Level 3	Interest Level 3–5

Other Books by Grahame
Wind in the Willows; Toad of Toad Hall; Ichabod and Mr. Toad

Information About the Author
Kenneth Grahame was born in Edinburgh, Scotland, in 1859. He lived in Great Britain all his life. In his earlier years he was a banker, and later he became an essayist, poet, and writer of children's books. He also loved to tell stories. The stories that he told his son at bedtime later became books for children. For example, one chapter he wrote for a book called *Dream Days* later became *The Reluctant Dragon*. Grahame used a lot of conversations between characters because he realized how much children enjoy talking with one another. His characters are friendly, and his books reflect his sense of humor. Mr. Grahame died in Pangbourne, England, in 1932.

Summary
This story is about a dragon, a boy, and a knight. The dragon is large and covered with shiny blue scales. He is a peaceful dragon who wants nothing to do with violence. The boy and the dragon become best friends. They share stories each evening. The knight is called on by the villagers to slay the dragon. The boy introduces the knight to the dragon, and together they plan to stage a "make-believe" slaying to satisfy the villagers. They succeed, and all live happily ever after.

Introduction
This story is called The *Reluctant Dragon*. "Reluctant" means unwilling. The dragon is called reluctant because he doesn't want to fight. Is there anything you are reluctant to do?

Key Vocabulary
shepherd	affable	gentry	stroll
meditate	wily	tyrant	audible
monotonous	occupation	valiant	culture
festal	noxious	scourge	

THE RELUCTANT DRAGON

Discussion Questions

1 Describe how the dragon looked. (Answers may vary but might include a description like "he was as big as four horses and covered with shiny deep-blue scales, shading off to a tender sort o' green below.")

2 How did the dragon explain his being? (He said the earth sneezed or shook itself or the bottom dropped out of something. So he scratched his way through a cave.)

3 What did the boy and the dragon like to do? (Answers may vary but might include telling stories, sharing poetry, and so on.)

4 Describe the village's festal appearance. (Carpets and gay-colored stuffs were hung out the windows, church bells clamored noisily, the little street was flower-strewn, and the whole population was chattering, shoving, and ordering one another back.)

5 Why did the villagers feel it was necessary to get St. George to come to their village? (Answers may vary but might include to slay the dragon and free them from him.)

6 Tell why the boy wanted St. George to meet the dragon. (Answers may vary but might include letting St. George see that he would like the dragon and would not want to hurt him.)

7 How did the dragon and St. George make the fight look real? (Answers may vary but might include the following: St. George pretended to stab him, the dragon romped and breathed fire, he lashed his long spiky tail, his claws tore up the turf, and so on.)

8 Would you have helped the dragon? Why or why not? (Answers may vary.)

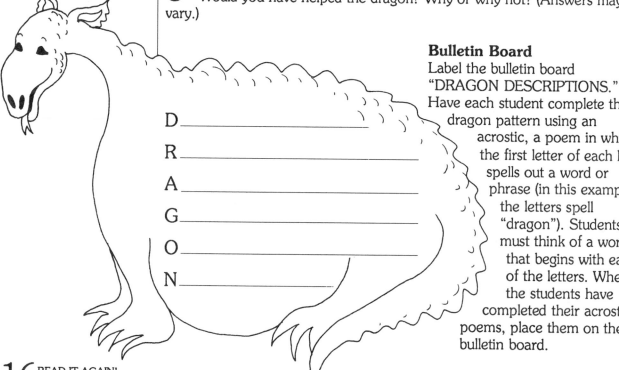

D _____

R _____

A _____

G _____

O _____

N _____

Bulletin Board

Label the bulletin board "DRAGON DESCRIPTIONS." Have each student complete the dragon pattern using an acrostic, a poem in which the first letter of each line spells out a word or phrase (in this example, the letters spell "dragon"). Students must think of a word that begins with each of the letters. When the students have completed their acrostic poems, place them on the bulletin board.

From *Read It Again: Book 2, A Guide for Teaching Reading Through Literature* published by Scott, Foresman and Company. Copyright © 1990 Liz Rothlein and Terri Christman.

THE RELUCTANT DRAGON

ACTIVITY SHEET 1

Directions

On the left, complete the bulletin describing the dragon slaying from the book *The Reluctant Dragon*. It took place hundreds of years ago. Next, pretend there is going to be a modern dragon slaying in your community. Using your imagination, complete the bulletin on the right.

Hear Ye, Hear Ye!
Come One, Come All
to a Dragon Slaying.
Date: Hundreds of Years Ago

Time: _____

Place: _____

Describe the event:

Attention! Attention!
BE SURE TO ATTEND THE
DRAGON SLAYING!

Date: _____

Time: _____

Place: _____

Describe the event:

THE RELUCTANT DRAGON

ACTIVITY SHEET 2

Name _____ Date _____

Directions

Sometimes people are stereotyped. A stereotype is an idea about a person, group, or thing that allows for no individuality. In *The Reluctant Dragon*, the dragon, the boy, and the knight do not fit the stereotype of most dragons, boys, and knights. On the left side, list the stereotypes for each of the characters. On the right, describe how they really are in the book.

Boys as they are stereotyped:

1. _____
2. _____
3. _____

Description of the boy in the story:

1. _____
2. _____
3. _____

Dragons as they are stereotyped:

1. _____
2. _____
3. _____

Description of the dragon in the story:

1. _____
2. _____
3. _____

Knights as they are stereotyped:

1. _____
2. _____
3. _____

Description of the knight in the story:

1. _____
2. _____
3. _____

Overall, which do you like better: the characters in the book the way they are or the way you stereotyped them? Explain.

_____

_____

From *Read It Again: Book 2, A Guide for Teaching Reading Through Literature* published by Scott, Foresman and Company. Copyright © 1990 Liz Rothlein and Terri Christman.

THE RELUCTANT DRAGON

Name _____ Date _____

Directions
Read the situation in each dragon. Decide who it would affect and what the effect would be by filling in the blanks.

What if St. George had not agreed to the "pretend" fight?
Who would it affect?

_____

What would the effect be?

_____

What if the dragon had gone back into the ground, never to be seen again?
Who would it affect?

_____

What would the effect be?

_____

What if the boy's parents had not let him visit the dragon?
Who would it affect?

_____

What would the effect be?

_____

What if St. George had made a mistake during the fight and stuck the sword in the wrong place?
Who would it affect?

_____

What would the effect be?

_____

20 READ IT AGAIN!
BOOK 2

From *Read It Again: Book 2, A Guide for Teaching Reading Through Literature* published by Scott, Foresman and Company. Copyright © 1990 Liz Rothlein and Terri Christman.

THE RELUCTANT DRAGON

Additional Activities

1 In *The Reluctant Dragon*, the boy becomes friends with the dragon by sharing poetry and stories. Discuss with students the importance of having friends and the qualities that make a good friend. Then have them get into small groups and decide how they would have approached the reluctant dragon so he would become their friend. Tell them to be creative!

2 The dragon in this story is very peaceful. He is not ferocious at all. He enjoys poetry and loves to tell stories. Yet he is as big as four horses and is covered with shiny deep-blue scales. Have the students complete this sentence: If I were a dragon, I would be _____. Then have them describe how they would look. Finally, ask the students to create an illustration portraying themselves as a dragon.

3 Talk to students about the term "peer pressure." In this story, the villagers want St. George to fight the dragon. They tell him he is a hero and bound to win. They also tell him he must fight for right and justice. Even after St. George finds out the dragon is nice, he still stages a "pretend" fight for the villagers. Ask students if they have ever felt "peer pressure." Have them describe what took place orally or in writing.

4 Discuss with students how the dragon, the boy, and the knight turn a violent situation into a peaceful situation. Using newspapers, have students locate articles with problem situations. Have them individually or in small groups come up with ideas for solving the problems in a peaceful way.

5 Have students draw "the reluctant dragon." Using the following directions for coloring rice, they can then make a mosaic dragon. Place rice in a jar and add a few drops of food coloring (amount depends on how light or dark you want the rice) and a capful of alcohol. Shake the jar until it is thoroughly mixed. Spread the rice on a newspaper to dry. Make a variety of colors so the dragons will be colorful.

6 Have students select a poem or story they feel would help them develop a friendship, as the boy and the dragon did. Provide opportunities for students to share their selections.

SARAH, PLAIN AND TALL

Author
Patricia MacLachlan

Publisher
Harper & Row, 1985

Pages 58	Reading Level 3	Interest Level 3–5

Other Books by MacLachlan
Arthur, for the First Time;
Cassie Binegar; Unclaimed
Treasures; The Sick Day;
Through Grandpa's Eyes;
Moons, Stars, Frogs, and
Friends; Mama One, Mama
Two; Tomorrow's Wizard.

Information About the Author
Patricia MacLachlan was born in Cheyenne, Wyoming. She is married and has three children. She has been an English teacher, lecturer, and teacher of creative writing workshops for adults and children. She started writing books when she was thirty-five years old. Mrs. MacLachlan recalls that the only story she wrote while she was in school turned out to be a disaster. She still remembers her teacher saying a story must have a beginning, middle, and ending—none of which her story had. She still has the story, which was about cats. She now emphasizes her family in her work. One of her books, *Sarah, Plain and Tall*, received the 1986 Newbery Medal award. This story is based on a person her mother knew. Mrs. MacLachlan wrote the story as a gift to her mother, who had Alzheimer's disease. She wanted to help her mother remember things from her past. Patricia MacLachlan currently lives in Massachusetts.

Summary
Papa places an ad in the newspaper for a wife. His first wife died while giving birth to their son Caleb. Papa also has a daughter, Anna. A woman from Maine named Sarah answers the ad. She and her cat, Seal, come to stay with them. However, everyone worries that Sarah misses too many things in Maine (the sea, her brother, and three aunts) and will return. Papa and the children do many things to try to make Sarah like their home as much as she likes her home in Maine. At the end of the story, Sarah takes the wagon to town alone. Papa and the children worry that she will not return, but she does. She tells them, "I will always miss my old home, but the truth of the matter is I would miss you more."

Introduction
In the story, *Sarah, Plain and Tall*, Sarah leaves her home in Maine. She misses the sea, her brother, and her three aunts. Think about how you would feel if you had to move. What and whom would you miss?

Key Vocabulary
dusk	hollow	familiar	horrid	wretched
murmur	chore	collapse	whickering	
pungent	eerie	squalls	stern	

SARAH, PLAIN AND TALL

From *Read It Again: Book 2, A Guide for Teaching Reading Through Literature* published by Scott, Foresman and Company. Copyright © 1990 Liz Rothlein and Terri Christman.

Discussion Questions

1 Anna tells us in the story that it took three days to love her new baby brother, Caleb. Why? (Answers may vary but might include the following: he was homely and plain, he had a terrible holler, he had a horrid smell, and their mama died the morning after his birth.)

2 Why do you think it is important to the children for Sarah to be able to sing? (Answers may vary but should have something to do with the fact that their deceased mother sang everyday.)

3 What does Sarah bring with her from Maine? (She brought Seal, the cat, shells, and a stone.)

4 Compare Sarah's dune and Papa's dune. (Answers may vary.)

5 What are some of the things Sarah does on the farm? (She plants and picks flowers, cooks, cuts hair, sings, draws pictures, plows fields, swims in the cow pond, feeds the chickens, drives a wagon, fixes a roof, takes care of sheep.)

6 How does Sarah bring the sea to Papa, Anna, and Caleb? (She creates a blue, gray, and green hanging for the wall.)

7 Explain what Sarah means when she says, "I will always miss my old home, but the truth of it is I would miss you more." (Answers may vary.)

8 If you were Sarah, would you stay on the farm or go back to Maine? Explain. (Answers may vary.)

Bulletin Board

Discuss with students the fact that in the story, *Sarah, Plain and Tall*, Sarah moves from Maine to a farm. When she moves she takes two things with her. She takes her cat, named Seal, and seashells. Ask students to identify five things they would take with them if they moved. Have them write these five things on the suitcase pattern and cut it out. Place the suitcases on the bulletin board, with the label "IF I MOVED I WOULD TAKE . . ."

NAME _____

1. _____

2. _____

3. _____

4. _____

5. _____

SARAH, PLAIN AND TALL

ACTIVITY SHEET 1

Name _____ Date _____

Directions

After hearing or reading *Sarah, Plain and Tall*, decide which part was the saddest, funniest, happiest, bravest, and best. Then illustrate each part in the space provided.

1. The saddest part was _____

   _____

   _____

   _____

2. The funniest part was _____

   _____

   _____

   _____

3. The happiest part was _____

   _____

   _____

   _____

4. The bravest part was _____

   _____

   _____

   _____

5. The best part was _____

   _____

   _____

   _____

Name _____ Date _____

**ACTIVITY
SHEET 2**

Directions

Below are things Sarah Elisabeth Wheaton does in the book *Sarah, Plain and Tall*. Read each statement and complete the questions below.

Sarah lived in Maine by the sea.
Sarah plants and picks flowers.
Sarah cooks.
Sarah cuts hair.
Sarah touches, talks, and runs with the lambs.

Sarah draws pictures.
Sarah swims in the cow pond.
Sarah feeds the chickens.
Sarah helps plow and plant in the fields.
Sarah drives the wagon to town alone.

What two things from Sarah's list would you like to do?

1. _____

Explain _____

2. _____

Explain _____

What two things from Sarah's list would you not like to do?

1. _____

Explain _____

2. _____

Explain _____

What are two more things Sarah does in the story?

1. _____

2. _____

Name_____ Date_____

Directions
Sarah moves from Maine to a farm. Moving can be very difficult. Before Sarah moves, she, Papa, and the children correspond to tell one another about where they live. The children tell Sarah their house is small and far out in the country, with no close neighbors. Think about someone moving into your community. What information would be helpful for them to know? Fill in the information below. Using the information, create a brochure about your community that could help someone feel more comfortable about moving. The outside of your brochure could be photographs or illustrations of your community.

**ACTIVITY
SHEET 3**

1. Describe your neighborhood._____
_____

2. Describe your school (size, location, and so on). _____
_____

3. What is the name of and location of the nearest hospital?_____
_____

4. What types of transportation are available?_____
_____

5. Where is the nearest library?_____

6. Where is the nearest park? _____
What is at this facility? _____

7. What sports are available?_____

8. What clubs exist? _____

9. List places of interest in your community. _____
_____

10. List other information that might be helpful for someone moving into your community. _____
_____

From *Read It Again: Book 2, A Guide for Teaching Reading Through Literature* published by Scott, Foresman and Company. Copyright © 1990 Liz Rothlein and Terri Christman.

SARAH, PLAIN AND TALL

Additional Activities

1 Discuss moving with the students. Ask them if they have ever moved and, if so, locate places where they have lived on the map. Talk about the feelings they experienced. Share books on the subject of moving, such as *Anything for a Friend*, by Ellen Conford, and *I Don't Live Here*, by Pam Conrad.

2 List on the chalkboard the two settings in *Sarah, Plain and Tall*: the farm and Maine. Do a semantic mapping or webbing of both settings to help students see the similarities and differences between the two environments. Tell students to fold a piece of paper (8½ × 11) in half. On one side they can create a picture of how they think the home on the farm looked and on the other side a picture of how they think Sarah's home in Maine looked. Allow time for students to share their perceptions of both settings.

3 Sarah likes to make charcoal drawings and send them home to Maine. She draws the fields, sheep, a windmill, Papa, Caleb sliding down a pile of hay, Anna in the bathtub, and so on. At the end of the story, she drives into town alone to get green, gray, and blue pencils. When Caleb sees the colored pencils, he says, "Sarah has brought us the sea!" Caleb says that because he knows Sarah is going to draw the sea. She hangs her drawing on the wall. Let students use blue, gray, and green colored pencils to draw the sea.

4 In this story, Papa places an advertisement in the newspaper for a wife. Tell students that people place ads in the newspaper for many reasons. Have them select an advertisement from the newspaper, cut it out, and stick it to a sheet of paper. Have students identify the purpose of their ad—is it to buy, sell, trade, advertise a service? Students could then design and write their own ad for something they have to buy, sell, or trade.

5 Explain to students that this story took place many years ago. Have them think about the types of transportation that were used. For example, Sarah says she walked from place to place when she lived in Maine. She takes a train to get from Maine to the town near the farm. Then Papa brings her to the farm in a wagon. Have students list all the forms of transportation they can think of that have existed over the years. Have them think about the forms of transportation that are yet to come. Next, ask them to select a way they would like to travel (from the past, present, or future) and tell where they would like to go. Also ask them to explain why they selected that particular mode of transportation.

THE WHIPPING BOY

Author
Sid Fleischman

Illustrator
Peter Sis

Publisher
William Morrow & Co., 1986

Pages 90	Reading Level 3	Interest Level 3–5

Other Books by Fleischman
*Mr. Mysterious and Company;
The Ghost in the Noonday Sun;
Longbeard the Wizard; The
Woodwen Cat Man; McBroom
Tells a Lie; McBroom and the
Beanstalk; Clancy and the
Grand Rascal; McBroom Tells
the Truth: Book World; Jingo
Django; Jim Bridger's Alarm;
Clock and Other Tall Tales;
The Ghost on Saturday Night;
Mr. Mysterious's Secrets of
Magic; Me and the Man on the
Moon-Eyed Horse*

Information About the Author
Sid Fleischman was born on March 16, 1920, in Brooklyn, New York. He is married and has three children. He lives in Santa Monica, California. At one time, Mr. Fleischman was a reporter. He also is a magician, screenwriter, and author of children's books. At the age of sixteen he went on tour doing magic shows. Mr. Fleischman is a master of the tall-tale adventure yarn and indicates he has no trouble finding ideas to write about. Yet he composes very slowly. He says it may take him five or six days to get one page the way he wants it. He likes to collect funny names and outrageous nicknames, which help him create the characters in his writings. He won the Newbery Medal in 1987 for *The Whipping Boy*, and his son won the Newbery Medal in 1989 for *Joyful Noise: Poems for Two Voices*.

Summary
This story is about Prince Brat and Jemmy. Prince Brat will someday be heir to the throne. In his kingdom it is forbidden to spank the heir to the throne. Therefore, Jemmy, an orphan boy, is kept in the castle to be punished in his place. Both boys dream of running away. When they do, their adventure provides them with many experiences that change their lives.

Introduction
In this story, Jemmy, the common boy, is spanked for everything Prince Brat does wrong (for example, he ties the lords' powdered wigs to the back of their chairs and he won't learn to read, write, and do sums). Which character would you want to be in this story? Why?

Key Vocabulary
prince	castle	guard	lantern	sewers	throne
villains	jewels	crown	soldiers	whip	saddle

THE WHIPPING BOY

From *Read It Again: Book 2, A Guide for Teaching Reading Through Literature* published by Scott, Foresman and Company. Copyright © 1990 Liz Rothlein and Terri Christman.

Discussion Questions

1 How do you feel about royal households of the past having whipping boys? What was the purpose for having a whipping boy? (Answers may vary.)

2 Why is Prince Horace called Prince Brat? (Answers may vary.)

3 Describe how Prince Brat and Jemmy feel about learning to read and write. (Answers may vary.)

4 Why does the Prince want to run away? (He is bored.)

5 What do Hold-Your-Nose Billy and Cutwater want as ransom for Prince Brat? (They want a cart full of gold and jewels.)

6 How does Jemmy feel about Prince Brat being whipped? (He had dreamed of seeing the prince whipped, but when it happens he finds no satisfaction in it.)

7 What are some of the kind things Captain Nips does for the runaways? (Answers may vary but might include giving them a ride, a place to hide, milk to drink, and potatoes to eat.)

8 Describe how both boys change during this story. (Answers may vary.)

Bulletin Board

In *The Whipping Boy*, Prince Brat and Jemmy run away. Have students trace their foot or shoe or provide them with a pattern to trace. On the cutout foot or shoe, have students complete this sentence: "I would like to run to _____ because _____." Then have them illustrate something they would see there. Title the bulletin board "RUNNING TO . . ."

Example:

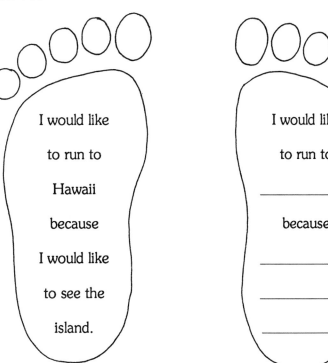

I would like to run to Hawaii because I would like to see the island.

I would like to run to _____ because _____ _____ _____

Name ———————————————————— Date ————————

Directions

Below is a list of some characters in *The Whipping Boy*. Place a check mark in each box that accurately describes the character.

Characters	Mischievous	Kind	Clever	Honest	Hard-working	Evil	Greedy	Friendly	Giving	Ugly	Sweet	Good
1. Prince Brat												
2. Jemmy												
3. King												
4. Hold-Your-Nose Billy												
5. Cutwater												
6. Betsy												
7. Captain Nips												
8. Smudge												

Select the character you feel is most like you. In the space provided, write a brief essay comparing yourself with that character.

I feel I am most like ——————————— because ————————————————

——————————————————————————————————

——————————————————————————————————

——————————————————————————————————

From *Read It Again: Book 2, A Guide for Teaching Reading Through Literature* published by Scott, Foresman and Company. Copyright © 1990 Liz Rothlein and Terri Christman.

Name _____ Date _____

From *Read It Again!: Book 2, A Guide for Teaching Reading Through Literature* published by Scott, Foresman and Company. Copyright © 1990 Liz Rothlein and Terri Christman.

**ACTIVITY
SHEET 2**

Directions

Prince Brat lives in a castle. Jemmy, the whipping boy, also lives in the castle. However, their bedrooms must be quite different. The author even tells you that Jemmy stays in a small chamber in the drafty north tower. Use your imagination to illustrate the two bedrooms.

Prince Brat's Bedroom

Jemmy's Bedroom

Which bedroom is most like yours? _____

Explain. _____

_____

_____

Name _____ Date _____

Directions

In *The Whipping Boy*, Cutwater and Hold-Your-Nose Billy kidnap Prince Brat and Jemmy. The captors have Jemmy (who they think is Prince Brat) write a ransom note. A ransom is a payment for the release of a person or property. This is what the note says:

> To the King's Most Sacred Majesty:
>
> Dear Papa,
>
> Our captors are loyal subjects, but scoundrels by trade. Don't cross them. They are shameful, mean, and rough as a sackful of nails. They fear no gallows. If they spy a single soldier's uniform, they'll crack my neck like a chicken's. They demand a ransom of a full cart of gold and jewels.
>
> Your Obedient Son,
>
> Prince Horace

Pretend you are in Jemmy's position and you have to write a ransom note for your captors. To whom would you write the ransom note?

_____

In the space provided below, write the ransom note.

_____

_____

_____

_____

From *Read It Again: Book 2, A Guide for Teaching Reading Through Literature* published by Scott, Foresman and Company. Copyright © 1990 Liz Rothlein and Terri Christman.

THE WHIPPING BOY

Additional Activities

1 The Newbery Medal was started in 1922 by Frederic Melcher, editor of *Publisher's Weekly* magazine. This award is a tribute to John Newbery, the first English publisher of books for children. It is given once a year to the author of the most distinguished contribution to children's literature. The author of *The Whipping Boy*, Sid Fleischman, was the 1987 recipient of this award. Select other Newbery Medal books and read them to students or have them read the books on their own. Ask them to explain, orally or in writing, why they feel the author was chosen, how the writing styles compare, and so on.

2 This story takes place centuries ago. Have students pretend they live in a time with castles and kings. If they could be a prince, what would they do? Ask students to describe, orally or in writing, their day as a prince. Allow the other students to comment on whether they would want each person to be a prince of the kingdom they lived in.

3 Have students play "Name That Prince." Each student should copy these sentences and fill in the blanks:

I know a prince,

All day long he _____.

His name is _____.

For example: I know a prince,
All day long he hops.
His name is Prince Bunny.

Give the students time to illustrate their prince doing what he does all day. Share them with the class.

4 Throughout this story, a friendship is developing. Have students discuss some of the events that create this friendship. Allow them to talk about the qualities a friend should have as you list the qualities on the chalkboard. Next, have students copy the list and number the qualities according to their importance. Finally, compare students' lists.

5 In this story both Jemmy and Prince Brat want to run away from the castle—but for different reasons. Discuss those reasons. The boys do end up running away together. Discuss the pros and cons of their running away.

6 Many people are kidnapped each year. Discuss important safety tips with the students. For example: Never accept a ride with a stranger. Discuss what Jemmy and Prince Brat should have done and what they do wrong when they are kidnapped. Have students design posters to help prevent kidnappings.

BRIDGE TO TERABITHIA

Author
Katherine Paterson

Publisher
Harper & Row, 1977

Pages 128	Reading Level 4	Interest Level 4–6

Other Books by Paterson
Jacob Have I Loved; The Great Gilly Hopkins; The Sign of the Chrysanthemum; Of Nightingales That Weep; The Master Puppeteer; Angels and Other Strangers; Family Christmas Stories; Star of Night; Consider the Lilies; Come Sing, Jimmy Jo; Rebels of the Heavenly Kingdom; The Crane Wife

Information About the Author
Katherine Womeldorf Paterson was born on October 31, 1932, in Quing Jiang, Jiangsu, China. As a child she first spoke Chinese. She came to the United States when she was five years old, and from that age until she was eighteen, she moved fifteen times. When she was a first grader in Richmond, Virginia, she came home on Valentine's Day without any valentines, because nobody knew her. This greatly troubled her mother, who many years later suggested that Katherine write a story about the day she received no valentines. Katherine responded, "But mother, all my stories are about the day I didn't get any valentines."

Katherine Paterson lives in Vermont. She has four children. Her husband, like her father, is a clergyman. Early in her life she was a teacher and a missionary. From 1964 on she authored many materials for church use, as well as books for young people. She has won many awards for her work. In 1978, she received both the Newbery Medal and the Lewis Carroll Shelf Award for her book *Bridge to Terabithia*. This book was written in response to the death of her son's best friend, Ellen, who was struck by lightning. Mrs. Paterson is currently working on two books, *The Mandarin Duck* and *The Spying Heart*.

Summary
This is a story about the friendship of Jess Aarons and Leslie Burke, who come from very different backgrounds. Together they create Terabithia, a magical kingdom in the woods. There the two of them reign as king and queen, and their imaginations set the only limits. However, one day a terrible tragedy occurs. Only when Jess comes to grips with this tragedy does he finally understand the strength and courage Leslie has given him.

Introduction
In this story, Jess Aarons and Leslie Burke find a special place of their own. They experience joys and sadness in their magical kingdom, called Terabithia. Do you have a place of your own where you can go and be in control? If not, have you ever wished for such a place?

Key Vocabulary
consolation	scrawny	realm
ominously	sporadically	predator
liberated	dignity	speculation

BRIDGE TO TERABITHIA

Discussion Questions

1 Why do you think Jess and Leslie create Terabithia? (Answers may vary.)

2 Why doesn't Leslie like living at Lark Creek? (Answers may vary but might include the fact that her lifestyle is very different; she has no TV, no friends; she can't do many of the sports she likes, such as gymnastics, and scuba diving.)

3 How do you think Leslie feels about her parents compared to how Jess feels about his? (Answers may vary but might include the fact that Leslie sees her parents less as authority figures than Jess does.)

4 How does Jess feel about his trip to Washington with Miss Edmunds? (Answers may vary but might include both joy and guilt.)

5 Why do you think Leslie wants to go to church with Jess's family on Easter? (Answers may vary.)

6 Why do you think Leslie doesn't have a TV at her house? (Answers may vary.)

7 Why do you think Jess builds the bridge to Terabithia? (Answers may vary but might include the following: so no one else would get hurt or because it no longer was a secret, sacred place to go.)

8 What do you think gives Jess the courage to say to Leslie, "I don't think it is safe to swing over to Terabithia when the water is so high. I am afraid"? (Answers may vary.)

Bulletin Board
Using large letters, put the following caption on the bulletin board: "[TEACHER'S NAME]'S [GRADE LEVEL] GRADE MAGICAL KINGDOM." After students complete Activity Sheet 1, ask them to draw a picture to illustrate the magical kingdom they have described. Put the illustrations, descriptions, and emblems for the magical kingdoms on the bulletin board.

Name _____ Date _____

Directions

Jess and Leslie create Terabithia, a special kingdom for themselves. Think about creating your own special kingdom. What would it be like? Where would it be? What would you call it? Who, if anybody, would be allowed into your kingdom? When would you go there? In the space, write a description of what your Terabithia would be like.

Directions

Countries, kingdoms, tribes, and families often have a crest or emblem to represent them. Using an encyclopedia, locate and read about the crests and emblems for the United States and England, as well as other countries in which you are interested. Now create a crest for the special kingdom you have described.

From *Read It Again! Book 2, A Guide for Teaching Reading Through Literature* published by Scott, Foresman and Company. Copyright © 1990 Liz Rothlein and Terri Christman.

Name _____ Date _____

From *Read It Again: Book 2, A Guide for Teaching Reading Through Literature* published by Scott, Foresman and Company. Copyright © 1990 Liz Rothlein and Terri Christman.

**ACTIVITY
SHEET 2**

Directions
Leslie and Jess come from very different family backgrounds and yet are able to build a strong friendship. In the spaces, list characteristics of each family that are different. For example, Jess's father works at any job available and his mother is a homemaker; Leslie's parents are both writers.

Jess's Family

Leslie's Family

_____

_____

_____

_____

_____

_____

_____

_____

_____

_____

Next, select a friend and list the differences between his or her family and your family.

Friend's Family

Your Family

_____

_____

_____

_____

_____

_____

_____

_____

What do you see as advantages of having friends from backgrounds different from your own?

_____

_____

What do you see as disadvantages of having friends from backgrounds different from your own?

_____

Name _____ Date _____

ACTIVITY
SHEET 3

Directions

Often the meaning of words can be figured out without using a dictionary. This is called using context clues. The following sentences are from *Bridge to Terabithia*. Using context clues, circle the word that best expresses the meaning of the underlined word. Finally, check the words you selected by looking up each of the underlined vocabulary words in the dictionary.

1. I am a <u>liberated</u> woman, Jess Aarons. When I invite a man out, I pay.

   oppressed   free   confined   open

2. It was raining off and on all day long. The rain continued <u>sporadically</u> as they tried to get to Terabithia.

   constantly   hesitantly   relentlessly   intermittently

3. If she was an animal predator, we'd be <u>obliged</u> to try to help her.

   indebted   happy   reluctant   anxious

4. The guardian of the <u>realm</u> raced about in happy circles.

   city   field   kingdom   area

5. Jess knew now that he would never be the best runner of the fourth and fifth grades, and his only <u>consolation</u> was that neither would Gary Fulcher.

   comfort   hope   happiness   difficulty

6. Mrs. Meyers' smile shifted suddenly and <u>ominously</u> into a scowl that silenced the class.

   calmly   wickedly   dangerously   lovingly

7. May Belle was as <u>scrawny</u> as Brenda was fat.

   pudgy   thin   muscular   hefty

8. "I will arise," he replied with <u>dignity</u>, "when thou removes this fool dog off my gut."

   honor   disgust   anger   resentment

9. This year Ellen and Brenda both had boyfriends at the <u>consolidated</u> high school and the problem of what to give them and what to expect from them was the cause of endless speculations and fights.

   gifted   neighborhood   unified   outdated

From *Read It Again: Book 2, A Guide for Teaching Reading Through Literature* published by Scott, Foresman and Company. Copyright © 1990 Liz Rothlein and Terri Christman.

BRIDGE TO TERABITHIA

From Read It Again: Book 2, A Guide for Teaching Reading Through Literature published by Scott, Foresman and Company. Copyright © 1990 Liz Rothlein and Terri Christman.

Additional Activities

1 Dealing with death is difficult. Discuss with the students how they feel about Leslie's death. Then provide them with a "Dear Abby" box in which they can put written messages, for you or for the guidance counselor, concerning their feelings about death. They may have concerns about the possible or actual death of someone close to them. Tell students that you or the guidance counselor will read the letters and respond to them with a private talk or a personal note.

2 Bring in a collection of newspapers that contain obituaries. Explain that an obituary is a published notice of death, usually including a brief biography of the deceased. Allow time for students to read at least two obituaries. Next, ask them to each write an obituary for Leslie. Then allow time for students to gather in small groups to compare their obituaries.

3 In the story, Jess could not afford to give Leslie a Christmas gift, and yet he wanted to give her something. One day he saw a sign for free puppies and decided that was the ideal gift for Leslie—which indeed it was! Ask students to think of the best gift they have ever received that was free or cost less than five dollars. Then identify a gift they have given that was free or cost less than five dollars. Discuss how these gifts compare to others they have given or received that cost more. Next, ask students to list the gifts they received for their last birthday, Christmas, or other occasion. Then ask them to list these gifts in order from favorite to least favorite. Finally, have them estimate the cost of each gift and determine if their favorite gifts were the most or least expensive.

4 If possible, provide a space in the classroom for students to develop a Terabithia. The students can brainstorm and then work collectively to design their own magic kingdom.

5 Many tombstones are inscribed with an epitaph. An epitaph describes, in very few words, the person who is buried there and his or her life. The following is an example of an epitaph:

Leslie Burke

Here lies her body, but her spirit remains a flame forever with others in Terabithia.

Tell students to think about Leslie and her life and then create an epitaph that would be appropriate for her.

6 Leslie loans Jess her books about Narnia so he can know more about magic kingdoms. Provide C. S. Lewis's well-known *The Chronicles of Narnia* for your students to read. After reading this series, discuss how these stories might have helped Jesse and Leslie create Terabithia.

7 If possible, obtain at least one of the following media materials for *Bridge to Terabithia*:

Listening record, cassette tape, or filmstrip with cassette tape (1978), Miller-Brody

Filmstrip (1980), Random House/Miller-Brody

Film (1985), PBS-TV

In class, compare the media materials with the actual book.

CHARLOTTE'S WEB

Author
E. B. White

Illustrator
Garth Williams

Publisher
Harper & Row, 1952

Pages 184	Reading Level 4	Interest Level 3–5

Other Books by White
Stuart Little; Trumpet of the Swan

Information About the Author

E. B. White was born on July 11, 1899, in Mt. Vernon, New York. His father was a piano manufacturer. E. B. White married an editor and had one child. He once said that he knew he had married the right woman when once they were packing and she said to be sure to put in the tooth twine. He said that anyone who called dental floss tooth twine was right for him.

As an adult, Mr. White moved to a farm in North Brooklin, Maine. On that farm he got the idea to write *Charlotte's Web*. One day when he was in the barn feeding his pig, he began feeling sorry for it because he knew it was doomed to die. Thinking of ways to save the pig, he came up with the idea for *Charlotte's Web*, which won a Newbery Honor Award in 1953.

In addition to writing books for children, Mr. White wrote books for adults. He also was a contributing editor to *The New Yorker* and wrote a monthly column for *Harper's* magazine. In 1963 he was named by President Kennedy as one of thirty-eight Americans to receive the Presidential Medal of Freedom. Mr. White died in October 1985 of Alzheimer's disease.

Summary

Wilbur, a runt pig, is lovingly raised by a girl named Fern. But once the pig grows, her parents make Fern sell the pig to her uncle, Mr. Zuckerman. He keeps Wilbur in the barn, where Wilbur meets his wonderful friend, Charlotte the spider, as well as other farm animals. Charlotte comes up with a clever idea to save Wilbur's life.

Introduction

Charlotte's Web is a story about a runt pig, Wilbur, that is saved from an early death by a little girl, Fern. As Wilbur grows bigger, he realizes that the farmer whose barn he lives in expects to kill him. In an attempt to save his life, Wilbur's good friend Charlotte, a beautiful gray spider, develops a clever plan. Read the story to find out if Charlotte's plan works. Or does Wilbur become someone's Christmas dinner?

Key Vocabulary

runt	radiant	scampered	thrashing	bloodthirsty
trough	terrific	mercilessly	exertions	detested

From *Read It Again: Book 2, A Guide for Teaching Reading Through Literature* published by Scott, Foresman and Company. Copyright © 1990 Liz Rothlein and Terri Christman.

CHARLOTTE'S WEB

Discussion Questions

1 Why do you think Mr. Arable, Fern's father, let Fern keep the runt pig instead of killing it? (Answers may vary.)

2 Which character in the story do you like best? Why? (Answers may vary.)

3 Do you think Fern will make a good parent when she grows up? Why or why not? (Answers may vary.)

4 Does Charlotte's writing words in the web make Wilbur any different kind of pig than if she hadn't written any words? Explain. (Answers may vary.)

5 Do you think Uncle, the big pig beside Wilbur at the fair, deserves to win the blue ribbon? Why or why not? (Answers may vary.)

6 Do you think Mrs. Arable should be so concerned about Fern's behavior that she goes to see Dr. Dorian about her? Why or why not? (Answers may vary.)

7 Which animal, other than Charlotte, do you feel is the wisest? Why? (Answers may vary.)

8 Why do you think Charlotte does so much for Wilbur? Explain. (Answers may vary.)

Bulletin Board

Cover the bulletin board with black construction paper. In large white letters, place the caption "LET'S SAVE WILBUR CAMPAIGN." Have students make a replica of a spider web with white yarn and thumbtacks, like this:

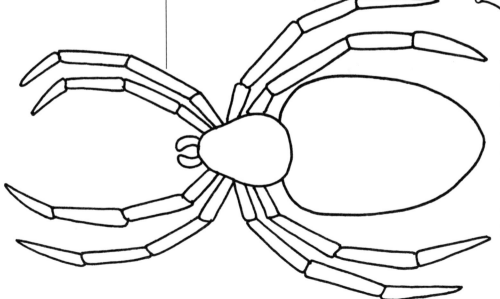

Duplicate the spider shape, and give one to each student. Have them write one or two words on their spider, words they think Charlotte might have spun in the web to help save Wilbur. Stick the spiders to the bulletin board.

Name _____ Date _____

Directions

Some of the things that happen in *Charlotte's Web* could actually happen in real life. Others could not and are considered make-believe. List five things from the story that could happen in real life and five things that could not happen in real life.

Things that <u>could</u> happen in real life.

1. _____

2. _____

3. _____

4. _____

5. _____

Things that <u>could not</u> happen in real life.

1. _____

2. _____

3. _____

4. _____

5. _____

Fact or Opinion

Just as some things are real and others are make-believe, some things are opinions and others are facts. A fact is something that can be proven—for example, palm trees grow in Florida. An opinion is something that can't be proven—for example, John's hair is <u>too</u> long. Read each of the following statements and put an *O* in the blank if it is an opinion or an *F* if it is a fact.

_____ 1. Charlotte is a spider.

_____ 2. Fern is kind to Wilbur.

_____ 3. Templeton is clever.

_____ 4. Wilbur goes to the fair.

_____ 5. Wilbur would be killed if it wasn't for Charlotte.

_____ 6. The old sheep is wise.

_____ 7. Wilbur likes to eat.

_____ 8. Charlotte makes webs.

From *Read It Again: Book 2, A Guide for Teaching Reading Through Literature* published by Scott, Foresman and Company. Copyright © 1990 Liz Rothlein and Terri Christman.

Name _____ Date _____

Directions

Answer the following questions in the spaces provided.

Charlotte is Wilbur's best friend. What does she do to earn such a friendship?

_____

_____

Likewise, Wilbur is Charlotte's best friend. What does he do to earn her friendship?

_____

_____

Identify the other characters that you consider friends of Wilbur, and explain why you believe this.

Character   Explanation

____ _____   _____

____ _____   _____

____ _____   _____

Next, place numbers to the left of each name to identify, in order, the most important friend to the least important friend.

Directions

Answer the following:

Who is your best friend? _____

What traits make this person your best friend?

_____

_____

Which of these traits is the most important to you when looking for a friend?

_____

Explain. _____

Name _____ Date _____

**ACTIVITY
SHEET 3**

Directions
Use science books, encyclopedias, or other appropriate reference books, such as *Spider Watching* by David Webster or *Discovering Spiders* by Malcolm Penny, to find the answers to the following questions:

1. To what classification of animals do spiders belong?_____

2. What other animals are included in this class?_____

3. Approximately how many different kinds of spiders are there?_____

4. What do spiders eat?_____

5. How do they get their food?_____

6. How often do they eat?_____

7. Where do they like to live?_____

8. Describe the body of a spider. Include the number of legs, eyes, body parts, and so on._____

    _____

9. Use the words in the box to label the parts of the spider:

legs
mouth parts
cephalothorax
abdomen
spinnerets

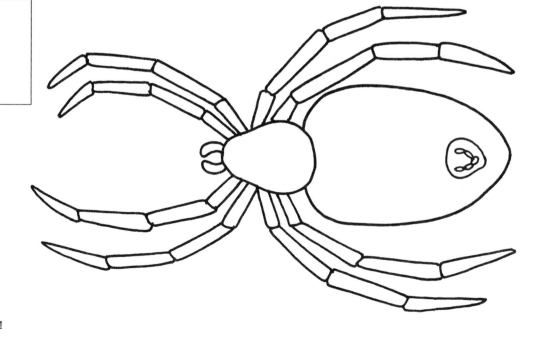

CHARLOTTE'S WEB

Additional Activities

1 Arrange a visit to a farm or a zoo with farm animals. Prior to the visit, give students an opportunity to read about the farm animals that are characters in *Charlotte's Web*. For example, find out what food products are obtained from the different animals; what their habitats are; what they eat. After the visit to the farm or zoo, let students compare what they saw with what they read about the animals in *Charlotte's Web* and in other books.

2 Tell students to go home and fill a spray bottle with water. Then they can look for spider webs. Tell them to *carefully* mist the web they find *lightly* with the water. The mist will help them see the web better. Then ask them to sketch the spider web. Display the web sketches so other students can see the similarities and differences.

3 After students have reviewed spiders and their habitats (Activity Sheet 3), cooperatively make a spider terrarium for the classroom. A terrarium can be made by placing some small pebbles, sand, and branches in a large, gallon jar with a cover that has tiny holes in it. Cautiously catch a spider to put into the terrarium. Remember that spiders do bite and that some of them are poisonous. Once the terrarium is established, feed the spider an insect; most spiders eat only once a month. Remind students to observe the spider on a daily basis.

4 If possible, go to a local fair and observe the animals and prizes. If that is not possible, discuss students' experiences at fairs. Compare their experiences with Fern and Avery's.

5 Ask students to write a short essay on what they might do to save Wilbur's life. Share the essays, and decide which student has the best idea.

6 Provide related books about friendship, such as *I Like You, You Like Me: Poems Of Friendship*, by Myra Cohn Livingston; *Your Former Friend, Matthew,* by Lou Ann Gaeddert; *The Gift*, by Helen Coutant. Encourage students to read at least one of these books. Compare the friendships in these books with the friendship between Charlotte and Wilbur in *Charlotte's Web*. Then, as a group, discuss what is expected from a good friend. Finally, ask each student to complete the following statement orally or in writing: "I believe a friend is someone who _____ ."

THE HUNDRED DRESSES

Author
Eleanor Estes

Illustrator
Louis Slobodkin

Publisher
Harcourt Brace, 1944

Pages 81	Reading Level 4	Interest Level 4–6

Other Books by Estes
The Moffits; The Middle Moffit; Rufus M; The Sun and the Wind and Mr. Toad; The Sleeping Giant; Ginger Pye; A Little Oven; Pinkey Pye; The Witch Family; Miranda the Great; The Echoing Green; The Alley; The Tunnel of Hugsy Goode; The Coat Hanger Christmas Tree

Information About the Author
Eleanor Estes was born on May 9, 1906, in West Haven, Connecticut. She is married and has one child. She has childhood memories of how wonderful West Haven was for growing up. There were trees to climb, places to fish, and big fields with daisies growing in them. She spent her first years of school in a small wooden schoolhouse. One of her books, *Ginger Pye*, the winner of the Newbery Medal, is about a dog that came to the window of that schoolhouse with a pencil in his mouth; she nicknamed him the "intellectual dog."

Early in her life, Mrs. Estes was a children's librarian. She now is a full-time writer who likes to make children laugh and cry and be moved in some way.

Summary
Each day Wanda Petronski comes to school in the same blue dress. The girls at school make fun of her. Wanda tells the girls that she has a hundred dresses in her closet at home. For a drawing contest at school, the boys design motor boats and the girls design dresses. Wanda draws a hundred dresses and wins the contest. However, by then Wanda has stopped coming to school. Her father has sent a note to the teacher explaining that they moved to a big city where people would not make fun of them. The girls, of course, feel bad for making fun of Wanda. They learn an important lesson.

Introduction
In this story, Wanda is a quiet little girl. She is poor and does not have much. In fact, she has only one blue dress that she wears to school every day. Also, she lives in Boggins Heights, which is not a good place to live. Her schoolmates make fun of her, which makes her feel very bad. If you went to school there, how could you help Wanda feel better?

Key Vocabulary
absence	dresses	waited	contest	hundred
laughing	drawings	school	teacher	popular
alone	friendship	feelings	closet	cruel

From *Read It Again: Book 2, A Guide for Teaching Reading Through Literature* published by Scott, Foresman and Company. Copyright © 1990 Liz Rothlein and Terri Christman.

THE HUNDRED DRESSES

Discussion Questions

1 Why does Wanda sit in the last seat in the last row in Room 13? (Answers may vary but might include the following: because she is quiet and rarely says anything at all; she is from Boggins Heights and her feet are caked with dry mud, so perhaps the teacher likes to keep all the children with dirty shoes in one corner of the room.)

2 Who is the most popular girl in school? Why? (Peggy is the most popular girl, because she is pretty, has attractive clothes, and has curly auburn hair.)

3 Describe Boggins Heights. (Answers may vary but might include the following: it was not a good place to live; it was a good place to pick flowers in the summer; old man Svenson lived there.)

4 In this story, when Wanda is asked to read a paragraph aloud, she sometimes won't read or, if she does, she takes forever. Why might Wanda do this? (Answers may vary but might include the following: she isn't very smart; she is timid; she needs to practice.)

5 Why do the Petronskis move to the big city? (They move so people won't notice them as much and make fun of them, because a city has a greater variety of all kinds of people than a small town does.)

6 How do the girls feel after hearing Miss Mason read the letter from Wanda's father? (Answers may vary but might include sorry, ashamed, sad, unhappy.)

7 Why do Maddie and Peggy go to see if Wanda has left town? (Answers may vary but might include the following: to tell her that she won the contest, that she is smart and the hundred dresses are beautiful, to apologize.)

8 What did you learn from reading *The Hundred Dresses*? (Answers may vary but might include to not make fun of anyone; to be kind to others; to have friends.)

Bulletin Board

Place "[TEACHER'S NAME]'S CLASS IS LOOKING GOOD" in big, bold white letters on the bulletin board. The backing should be black. Give each student a sheet of white paper (11½ × 14) and magazines. Have students cut out pictures of shoes, skirts, pants, blouses, dresses, shirts, earrings, and other clothing or accessories until they have enough to fully dress a person. They can then glue the pictures on the sheet of paper and draw themselves in these clothes (head, arms, legs). Put the finished pictures on the bulletin board.

Name _____ Date _____

Directions

When they play the dress game, Wanda tells the girls she has a hundred dresses hanging in her closet. Below in three of the squares are descriptions of some of her dresses. Illustrate a dress for each of these descriptions. The last square is empty so you can design a dress and write its description.

1.	2.
The dress in the picture Wanda gives Peggy is green with red trimming. It is velvet and floor length.	The dress in the picture Wanda gives Maddie is blue with red trim. It is silk and floor length.

3.	4.
The dress Wanda wears to school each day is blue. It is knee length and cotton.	_____ _____ _____

From *Read It Again: Book 2, A Guide for Teaching Reading Through Literature* published by Scott, Foresman and Company. Copyright © 1990 Liz Rothlein and Terri Christman.

Name _____ Date _____

From *Read It Again: Book 2, A Guide for Teaching Reading Through Literature* published by Scott, Foresman and Company. Copyright © 1990 Liz Rothlein and Terri Christman.

ACTIVITY SHEET 2

Directions

In *The Hundred Dresses*, Maddie and Peggy write a friendly letter to Wanda telling her she has won the contest and how pretty her drawings are. They tell her they are studying about Winfield Scott. They ask her about her new home and her new teacher. They mean to tell her they are sorry, but they never do. If you were writing Wanda a letter, what would you say to her? Fill in the friendly letter form below.

Date

Greeting,

_____

_____

_____

_____

_____

Body

_____

_____

_____

_____

_____

_____

Closing,

Signature

Name _____ Date _____

Directions

Often, just as in the story, people say or do things that have an effect on the way another person feels. Read each of the following situations. Describe how you would feel—happy, sad, angry, proud, ashamed, lonely, okay, scared, and so on—and what you would do in each situation. Then draw a face in the circle to match the feeling.

ACTIVITY SHEET 3

You are in art class. The teacher's assignment is to draw what you like best. When everyone is finished, the teacher asks each person to share his or her drawing. When you hold yours up, no one seems to like it.

How would you feel? _____

What would you do? _____

You are shopping with your mother. You see a toy like one your friend has. You really want to have it. But your mother says no.

How would you feel? _____

What would you do? _____

Your teacher has asked each student to pick a poem, memorize it, and present it to the class. It is your turn to recite your poem.

How would you feel? _____

What would you do? _____

Your best friend doesn't feel well, and she can't play with you. There is nothing to watch on television. Your family is busy working around the house and not paying much attention to you.

How would you feel? _____

What would you do? _____

You are walking home from school. You find a wallet. When you get home your parents call the police. The wallet is returned to the owner, who is very grateful.

How would you feel? _____

What would you do? _____

From *Read It Again: Book 2, A Guide for Teaching Reading Through Literature* published by Scott, Foresman and Company. Copyright © 1990 Liz Rothlein and Terri Christman.

THE HUNDRED DRESSES

Additional Activities

1 One of the things the girls make fun of is Wanda's name: Petronski. They yell, "Petronski–Onski!" Have students create a family tree for themselves, indicating from which country each family member originated. Once they find out about their family's origin, have them place their last name on an index card (5 × 7), along with a photograph of them or their family. Place a world map on the wall. Arrange all the index cards around the map. Then have students place one end of a piece of yarn on the country and the other end on their index card. Discuss the variety of names, as well as the idea that certain names are considered typical of a particular country.

2 In *The Hundred Dresses*, Mr. Petronski sends a letter to the class, Maddie and Peggy send a letter to Wanda, and Wanda sends a letter to the class. This is an excellent time to invite a mail carrier to come to class. He or she could discuss how to become a postal worker, the various positions, the duties, and what the job is like.

3 This would also be a good time to have students practice addressing envelopes. Give each student an envelope. Tell students to write their address on the envelope. Then put all the envelopes into a box. Ask each student to take one envelope without looking. Finally, tell students to write a friendly letter to the person whose name and address appears on the envelope and then to mail the letter.

4 Invite your school counselor into your classroom. Have students discuss the story with the counselor. The counselor can then talk to the students about friendship and feelings. Perhaps students can then make a "Wanda mobile." Write Wanda's name on a large piece of paper and attach it to a piece of yarn hanging from the center of a hanger. On smaller pieces of paper, have students write words identifying how they think Wanda feels in the story. Hang these from the hanger using pieces of yarn. For example: Next have the students create a mobile depicting their own qualities or characteristics.

5 Mr. Petronski, Wanda's father, writes a letter telling everyone his family has moved to a big city. Have students write a creative paragraph about where they think Wanda and her father have moved (what city), what it is like, what their house looks like, what her new school and teacher are like, whether Wanda has friends, and so on. Let students share their paragraphs with the rest of the class. Discuss how different or similar the paragraphs are.

6 Ask students to select five criteria they would use in choosing a new location to live in. Next, have them research various cities or localities to find the one that best fits their criteria. Finally, they can write a brief paragraph describing what they think their life would be like in this new place. Provide time for students to share these paragraphs with one another.

JAMES AND THE GIANT PEACH

Author
Roald Dahl

Illustrator
Nancy Ekholm Burkert

Publisher
Alfred A. Knopf, 1961

Pages 154	Reading Level 4	Interest Level 4–6

Other Books by Dahl
Danny the Champion of the World; The Wonderful Story of Henry Sugar; Charlie and the Chocolate Factory; The Enormous Crocodile; Fantastic Mr. Fox; The Twits; Charlie and the Great Glass Elevator; The Gremlins; Magic Finger

Information About the Author
Roald Dahl (pronounced Roo-aal) was born on September 13, 1916, in Llandoff, South Wales. He is married and has three children. He was a freelance writer, served in the military, and later became a writer of children's books as well as adult novels. It was only because of reading stories to his children that he became interested in writing children's books. He found it difficult to find any books that really excited his children; thus he decided to tell them his own stories, which he then made into books. He currently lives in Buckinghamshire, England.

Summary
This story is about a young orphan boy named James (his parents were eaten by an angry rhinoceros). He has to live with his Aunt Sponge and Aunt Spiker, who are cruel to him. One day, a small, old man gives James a bag of magic that is supposed to make his life marvelous. However, James accidentally drops the bag of magic under a peach tree. The magic creates an enormous peach. One night James enters the peach. Once inside, he finds bugs that are also affected by the magic. James and his bug friends then begin a series of unusual and exciting adventures.

Introduction
James Henry Trotter is orphaned when he is four years old. His mother and father go to London to do some shopping and are eaten by an enormous, angry rhinoceros that escaped from the London Zoo. James then has to live with his mean Aunt Sponge and Aunt Spiker. He misses his happy life with his parents. He misses his house by the sea. He misses all the children he played with. If you had to leave your home, what things would you miss?

Key Vocabulary

nuisance	ancient	luminous	hideous	mammoth
famished	lurch	insidiously	pandemonium	hailstones
loathsome	enthralled	gape	malevolently	

From *Read It Again: Book 2, A Guide for Teaching Reading Through Literature* published by Scott, Foresman and Company. Copyright © 1990 Liz Rothlein and Terri Christman.

JAMES AND THE GIANT PEACH

From *Read It Again: Book 2, A Guide for Teaching Reading Through Literature* published by Scott, Foresman and Company. Copyright © 1990 Liz Rothlein and Terri Christman.

Discussion Questions

1 Explain why James is sent to live with Aunt Sponge and Aunt Spiker. (His parents have been eaten by an enormous, angry rhinoceros.)

2 Compare James's past life with his parents to his present life with Aunt Sponge and Aunt Spiker. (Answers may vary.)

3 What does the little old man tell James to do with the bag of magic? (He says to take a large jug of water and pour all the little green things into it; then, slowly add ten hairs from his own head; finally, drink the whole jugful in one gulp.)

4 Describe the friends James meets in the giant peach. (Answers may vary.)

5 Who helps get the peach out of the ocean? How do they help? (Answers may vary.)

6 How do the Cloudmen make hailstones? (Answers may vary.)

7 Describe all the nice things that happen to James and his friends once they land in New York City. (Answers may vary.)

8 Why was this story written? (So many children begged James to tell the story of his adventures in the peach that he thought it would be nice to sit down and write a book.)

Bulletin Board

Remind students that in this story a small old man in a crazy, dark-green suit emerges from the bushes. He takes out a small white paper bag and hands it to James. Inside the bag is a mass of tiny green things that look like little stones. The old man tells James there is power and magic in them.

Give each student a lunch-size paper bag. Have them place beans, stones, peas, or something else inside their bag to make it a bag of magic. On the outside of the bag, have each student describe what is in the magic bag, what makes the magic work, and what it does. You can then staple all of the paper bags to the bulletin board. Label the bulletin board "OUR BAGS OF MAGIC."

Name _____ Date _____

Directions

Each illustration represents an event in *James and the Giant Peach*. Describe each event, and place the events in the correct order by numbering them from 1 to 5.

____   _____

_____

_____

____   _____

_____

_____

____   _____

_____

_____

____   _____

_____

_____

____   _____

_____

_____

From *Read It Again: Book 2, A Guide for Teaching Reading Through Literature* published by Scott, Foresman and Company. Copyright © 1990 Liz Rothlein and Terri Christman.

JAMES AND
THE GIANT
PEACH

**ACTIVITY
SHEET 2**

Name _____ Date _____

Directions

Read all the words in the peach. They are all words that
describe the characters listed below. Select the words that
best describe each character and place them under the
character's name. You may use the words more than once.

James Henry Trotter

_____   _____

_____   _____

Aunt Sponge

_____   _____

_____   _____

Grasshopper

_____   _____

_____   _____

Centipede

_____   _____

_____   _____

Silkworm

_____   _____

_____   _____

Glowworm

_____   _____

_____   _____

Ladybug

_____   _____

_____   _____

Man

_____   _____

_____   _____

Aunt Spiker

_____   _____

_____   _____

Spider

_____   _____

_____   _____

Earthworm

_____   _____

_____   _____

horrible   selfish
lazy   lots of legs   lady firefly
green light   blind   male
old   female   cruel   lonely
short   small eyes   pest
black glassy eyes   sunken mouth
flabby face   spinner   bony
hero   friendly   short horns
two feelers   worker   nine-spotted
sharp jaws   screechy voice   vain
white   thinker   small
musician   thick   bald head
sad   insect
human   green   enormous
nice   pink skin   fat
tall   lean   big

Name _____ Date _____

Directions

Below are four events from *James and the Giant Peach*. Read each event and predict what might have happened if the event were changed. A prediction is what one believes will happen; there are no right or wrong answers.

1.   Aunt Spiker and Aunt Sponge are very mean to James. They never call James by his real name. Instead, they call him things like "you miserable creature" and "you disgusting little beast." He never gets any toys. They don't allow him to go anywhere or have friends. He works hard. Predict what James's life would be like if Aunt Spiker and Aunt Sponge were nice to him.

Prediction: _____

_____

_____

_____

2.   A small, old man in a crazy, dark-green suit gives James a small white paper bag full of little green stone-like things. He tells James to take a large jug of water and pour the little green things into it. Slowly, one by one, he is to add ten hairs from his head. Then he is to drink the jugful in one gulp. Immediately after that, fabulous things are supposed to happen. However, James drops the bag, and the magic power goes into the ground beneath a peach tree. Predict what would have happened to James if he had drunk the jugful of magic.

Prediction: _____

_____

_____

_____

From *Read It Again: Book 2, A Guide for Teaching Reading Through Literature* published by Scott, Foresman and Company. Copyright © 1990 Liz Rothlein and Terri Christman.

3.   The giant peach ends up rolling into the sea. James and the creatures can tell they are in the sea because they are bobbing up and down. Lots of sharks begin to attack the peach. James comes up with a plan that lifts the giant peach out of the water. Predict what would have happened to the giant peach, James, and his friends if the plan had not worked.

Prediction: _____

_____

_____

_____

4.   People in New York City see the giant peach hovering overhead. They think it is the biggest bomb in the history of the world. The giant peach eventually lands on top of the Empire State Building. Slowly, everyone comes out of the peach. They all become heroes and are given a parade. They all become rich and successful in the new community. Predict what would have happened to James and his friends had the giant peach landed somewhere else—for example, the Great Wall of China, the Tower of London, or Niagara Falls.

Prediction: _____

_____

_____

_____

Additional Activities

1 James and his friends have quite an adventure in the peach. Below are a few delicious peach recipes you may want to try with your students. Remember, peaches in yogurt and jello are delicious and easy to do with your students.

Peach Cooler

1½ c. peeled and sliced peaches
⅓ c. apple juice concentrate
1¼ c. milk

Place all the ingredients in a blender and purée. Chill before serving. Makes 1 serving.

Peach Cobbler

8 fresh peeled and sliced peaches   1½ tsp. cinnamon
½ c. apple juice concentrate   2 tsp. margarine
1¼ c. Grapenuts

Stir peaches and apple juice concentrate together. Place the mixture in a 9 × 12 greased pan. In another bowl mix the Grapenuts and cinnamon; sprinkle over the peach mixture. Dot the margarine on top. Bake at 350° for 30 minutes. Makes approximately 12 servings.

---

2 Share some newspaper articles with your students or allow them to browse on their own. Discuss with them how an article covers the basic facts: who, what, when, where, why, and how. Have students write about the giant peach coming to New York City. The headline might be "Giant Peach Lands on Empire State Building." Each article should cover who, what, when, where, why, and how. Students may want to attach an illustration. Finally, share the headlines and articles aloud.

3 Discuss with students how the peach tree and the creatures receive the full magic from the little old man's bag of magic. Once they receive the magic, they become enormous. Have the students think about who or what they would like to see get enormous and why. Then have them complete this sentence: "I would like to see _____ get enormous because _____. Let students illustrate their sentence. Share these projects aloud with the class.

4 Place a world map on the chalkboard. Using construction paper, create a small peach. Put a piece of tape on the back. Have students take turns coming up and placing the peach on different continents, countries, oceans, and so on. The class can describe what the peach would see in each location.

From *Read It Again: Book 2, A Guide for Teaching Reading Through Literature* published by Scott, Foresman and Company. Copyright © 1990 Liz Rothlein and Terri Christman.

RAMONA THE PEST

Author
Beverly Cleary

Publisher
Dell Publishing, 1968

Pages 192	Reading Level 4	Interest Level 4–6

Additional Books by Cleary
Dear Mr. Henshaw; Beezus and Ramona; Ellen Tebbits; Emily's Runaway Imagination; Henry Huggins; Henry and Beezus; Henry and the Clubhouse; Henry and the Paper Route; Henry and Ribsy; Mitch and Amy; The Mouse and the Motorcycle; Otis Spofford; Ramona and Her Father; Ramona and Her Mother; Runaway Ralph; Socks; Ramona Quimby, Age 8; Ramona Forever

Information About the Author
Beverly Cleary was born in Oregon in 1916. She lived in a thirteen-room farmhouse that was built by pioneers. She was first introduced to books by her mother, who started the first library in a nearby town. When she was six years old, her family moved from the farm to the city, and her life changed drastically. She didn't like school until she was in the third grade. It was then that she first enjoyed reading.

Ms. Cleary, a librarian, has based many of her stories on what she enjoyed as a child. Her books contain humor about real-life problems that children experience. One of her books, *Dear Mr. Henshaw*, won the Newbery Medal in 1984, and in 1982 *Ramona Quimby, Age 8* won the Newbery Honor Book Award. She has also received the Laura Ingalls Wilder Award.

Summary
This story is about a lovable five-year-old girl who is very excited because she has just entered kindergarten. Ramona is considered a pest because she is curious about life and tends to do things that annoy other people. She believes school is fun until suddenly she almost becomes a kindergarten dropout.

Introduction
Things you do can sometimes bother other people, or things other people do can bother you. In this story, Ramona is considered a pest. Can you think of any time when you are or have been a pest? As you read the story, think about the things Ramona does and decide if Ramona is a pest or not.

Key Vocabulary

intersection	enticingly	contradicted
reproachfully	infuriated	ferocious
gloated	indignant	predicament

RAMONA THE PEST

Discussion Questions

1 Do you think Ramona is a pest? Why or why not? (Answers may vary.)

2 Do you think the principal, Miss Mullen, should punish Ramona for hiding behind the trash can? Why or why not? (Answers may vary.)

3 How does Ramona finally get a pair of red boots? (She outgrows her neighbor's, Howie's, old pair of boots.)

4 Select one "pesty" event for which Ramona is responsible. Explain what happens. (Answers may vary.)

5 Who do you think is Ramona's best friend? Explain. (Answers may vary but might include Henry Huggins or Miss Binney.)

6 Why do you think Ramona decides to go back to kindergarten after she says she isn't going back? (Answers may vary but might include the nice note from Miss Binney or being scared of the truant officer or being bored staying home.)

7 Do you think it is wise for Ramona's mother and father to let her decide, on her own, to return to kindergarten? Explain. (Answers may vary.)

8 Would you like to have someone like Ramona as a friend? Why or why not? (Answers may vary.)

Bulletin Board

In large letters, put the caption "AM I REALLY A PEST?" on the bulletin board. Tell students that everyone is a pest at one time or another. In other words, we sometimes do things that bother other people. Ask students to think of something they do that might bother someone else and then develop a "Pest Poster," as described below. On completion of the "Pest Poster," tell students to hang them on the bulletin board. Finally, let others sign if they agree that the person is a pest when he or she does what is described.

Name _____

I am a pest when _____

_____

_____

Signed _____

I agree that [student's name] is a pest when he/she does what is described above.

Signatures

_____   _____

_____   _____

From *Read It Again: Book 2, A Guide for Teaching Reading Through Literature* published by Scott, Foresman and Company. Copyright © 1990 Liz Rothlein and Terri Christman.

Name _____ Date _____

Directions

Read each sentence. Circle the code letter below to show whether the sentence is true or false. For example, the first statement, "Ramona believes that she is a pest," is false. Therefore, under the numeral 1 below, you would circle the letter "E."

**ACTIVITY
SHEET 1**

1. Ramona believes that she is a pest.
2. On the first day of school, Ramona does not want to walk with Beezus and Mary Jane.
3. Ramona thinks that her kindergarten teacher, Miss Binney, is going to give her a present for staying in her seat.
4. Miss Binney chooses Ramona to be the wake-up fairy on the first day of school.
5. The class giggles when Ramona says her doll's name is Chevrolet.
6. Ramona likes Susan's curls.
7. Ramona likes walking to school with Howie and his mother.
8. The principal, Miss Mullen, punishes Ramona for hiding behind the trash cans.
9. Ramona leaves her tooth with Miss Binney.

	1	2	3	4	5	6	7	8	9
True	M	R	U	T	N	G	J	A	Y
False	(E)	P	O	H	Y	L	I	S	W

Directions

Write the circled letters in the blanks below to find out the name of one of the characters in the story. For example, the first statement is false, and therefore the letter "E" is circled and the letter "E" is written above the numeral 1.

___ _E_ ___ ___ ___   ___ ___ ___ ___ ___ ___ ___
 4   1   5   2   9   4   3   6   6   7   5   8

Name _____ Date _____

Directions
Remember your first day in kindergarten by answering the following questions:

1. What one thing do you remember most about your first day in kindergarten?

_____

2. How did you feel about being at school? _____

   Why? _____

3. What was the teacher like? _____

4. What was his or her name? _____

5. What did you like best about kindergarten? _____

_____

   Why? _____

6. What did you like least about kindergarten? _____

_____

   Why? _____

The following provides you with an example of the cinquain form of poetry and a sample cinquain poem. In the space provided, write a cinquain poem describing something about your experiences in kindergarten.

Cinquain Poetry Form	**Sample Cinquain Poem**
Line 1: one word (may be the title)	Teacher
Line 2: two words (describing the title)	Very nice
Line 3: three words (an action)	Read good books
Line 4: four words (a feeling)	Was always very understanding
Line 5: one word (referring to the title)	Caring

_____

_____

_____

_____

_____

From *Read It Again: Book 2, A Guide for Teaching Reading Through Literature* published by Scott, Foresman and Company. Copyright © 1990 Liz Rothlein and Terri Christman.

Name _____ Date _____

Directions

Pretend that you are an advice columnist like Ann Landers or Dear Abby. Read each of the following letters and decided what advice you would give to Ramona so she won't be considered a pest. In the space provided, write Ramona a letter giving your advice.

Dear Abby,

Today I went to school, and my kindergarten teacher, Miss Binney, was not there. I do not feel like going into the room with the substitute. What should I do?

Love, Ramona

_____
_____
_____

Dear Abby,

I pulled Susan's hair because she said I was a big pest. Miss Binney said that if I can't stop pulling Susan's hair, I will have to go home and stay there until I can stop. I don't want to stop pulling Susan's hair. What should I do?

Love, Ramona

_____
_____
_____

Dear Abby,

Every morning when I go to school, I chase Davy because I want to kiss him, but he won't let me. What should I do?

Love, Ramona

_____
_____
_____

Additional Activities

1 Pair your students with a group of kindergarten children. Allow the kindergarten children time to discuss their experiences as a kindergarten student with their partners. Following the discussions, allow time for the kindergarten children to dictate stories about their kindergarten experiences as your students write down what they say. Your students may want to use Activity Sheet 2 as a questionnaire, especially for children who do not have much to say. As a culmination to this activity, have a book-making session, using the directions for making a book found in the appendix. Note: Include illustrations and/or photographs in the book.

2 When Ramona writes the first letter of her last name, a "Q," she decorates it and makes it into a cat. Ask students to use the last letter of their names to create a design, animal, or other picture.

3 Discuss with students the concept of being a pest. Ask what they believe a pest is. Look up "pest" in the dictionary, and write the definition on the chalkboard. Discuss the things Ramona does that make her a pest. Finally, ask students to create a humorous book titled *[Student's name], the Pest*. In this book, students should write fictitious, humorous things they might do that would make them a pest. Tell them to illustrate the book and make a cover.

4 Many things that happen could be considered "pesty." For example, a heavy rain when you want to have a picnic is a pest. Provide local newspapers for the students. Ask them to clip headlines of events that could be considered "pesty." Have each student make a collage of his/her headlines, gluing them on a sheet of paper. Allow time for students to discuss their headlines with other students.

5 Read *Ramona Quimby, Age 8* and the other Ramona books by Beverly Cleary, which follow Ramona as she and her family grow older and experience the changes and challenges of life. Compare these books with *Ramona the Pest*.

6 Encourage students to write a short story about their first days of school, using the information provided on Activity Sheet 2 plus additional information, such as kindergarten pictures and samples of schoolwork. Provide time to share these stories.

7 Ask students to bring in a photograph of themselves when they were in kindergarten. Display these pictures on the bulletin board. Then ask students to analyze the similarities and differences in the way they looked then and how they look today—for example, length of hair and height.

From *Read It Again: Book 2, A Guide for Teaching Reading Through Literature* published by Scott, Foresman and Company. Copyright © 1990 Liz Rothlein and Terri Christman.

CALL IT COURAGE

Author
Armstrong Sperry

Publisher
Macmillan, 1940

Pages 116	Reading Level 5	Interest Level 4–6

Other Books by Sperry
Wagon Westward; Danger to Windward; South of Cape Horn; Storm Canvas; One Day With Manu; One Day With Jambi; One Day with Tuktu; All Sail Set; Little Eagles; Lost Lagoon

Information About the Author
Armstrong Sperry was born on November 7, 1897, in New Haven, Connecticut. He was married and had two children. He was an author and an illustrator of children's books for ten years before combining his illustrations with his own works. He spoke French and Tahitian and spent two years in the French-owned islands in the South Pacific. He spent most of his adult life living in New Hampshire, although he traveled extensively, exploring the South Sea islands, Europe, the West Indies, and the United States. His travels and his grandfather's tales of South Seas adventures inspired his books. He won the Newbery Medal for *Call It Courage*. He died on April 28, 1976, in Hanover, New Hampshire.

Summary
A Polynesian chief's son, Mafatu, whose name means Stout Heart, is called a coward by the people of his island. He fears the sea because it killed his mother when he was a baby. At the age of ten, Mafatu can no longer bear the taunts and jibes about his fears, so he paddles out to sea, alone in his canoe, to conquer his fear.

Introduction
Call It Courage is a fictitious story about Mafatu, the "boy who is afraid." Mafatu's will to be courageous leads him to the sea to conquer his fear of it. Have you ever wished for the courage to do something? If so, to what extent have you developed courage? As you read the story about Mafatu, think about what he does to develop courage compared to what you might need to do.

Key Vocabulary
plateau	shoaled	impending	eternal	deference
irresolute	chants	indifference	despairing	impaled
haunches	premonition			

CALL IT COURAGE

Discussion Questions

1 Why does Mafatu fear the sea? (The sea killed his mother when he was a baby.)

2 What happens that makes Mafatu set out on his quest, alone, to conquer his fear? (Answers may vary but may include that he hears Kana, his friend, say he is a coward or that he feels he has to live up to his father's expectations and his name, which means Stout Heart.)

3 How do you think Mafatu would have felt if the hammerhead shark had killed Uri and he had stood by and watched? (Answers may vary but may include guilty or cowardly.)

4 At what point in the story do you think Mafatu starts feeling differently about himself? (Answers may vary.)

5 What are at least three things Mafatu does that give him confidence and help develop his courage? (Answers may vary but might include killing the hammerhead, wild boar, and octopus; crossing the ocean in the storm; providing food, clothing, and shelter for himself and his dog on the island.)

6 What do you think Mafatu's life would have been like if he had not done what he did? (Answers may vary.)

7 Which of Mafatu's accomplishments actually relate to overcoming his fear of the sea? (Answers may vary.)

8 What do you think Kana and Mafatu's relationship will be like now that he has returned from his adventure? (Answers may vary.)

Bulletin Board

Put the caption "COURAGEOUS DEEDS" in large letters across the bulletin board. Then discuss the courage Mafatu exhibits in this story plus other courageous events that students may have read about or experienced. Tell them that often courageous deeds are written about in newspapers and magazines. Ask students to scan publications to find articles about individuals or groups of people who have performed courageous deeds. Instruct them to cut out these articles and bring them into the classroom to put up on the bulletin board. Every few days, allow time for students to share their articles about courageous deeds.

From *Read It Again: Book 2, A Guide for Teaching Reading Through Literature* published by Scott, Foresman and Company. Copyright © 1990 Liz Rothlein and Terri Christman.

**ACTIVITY.
SHEET 1**

Name _____ Date _____

Directions

In the word search below, find the words used by the people of Hikueru, a Polynesian island in the South Seas.

tupapau	pareu	puaa	Moana	tamanu	pahua
Mafatu	Maui	feke	coir	marae	mape
bonitos	purau	fei			

```
P  O  I  U  Y  T  R  E  W  M  B
M  T  U  P  A  P  A  U  S  A  D
D  O  F  G  M  J  A  L  K  F  E
Z  C  A  V  B  A  B  R  M  A  G
P  W  E  N  R  M  P  U  A  T  I
A  S  D  F  A  A  J  E  L  U  J
R  M  N  C  B  U  M  A  R  A  E
E  M  B  O  N  I  T  O  S  P  M
U  G  A  I  K  L  H  D  M  T  N
H  K  P  R  W  J  P  U  R  A  U
Q  W  M  A  A  N  U  D  P  M  P
F  E  I  T  H  E  A  F  E  A  Q
E  S  D  F  G  U  A  H  C  N  R
K  Z  M  A  U  I  A  J  A  U  S
E  M  A  S  T  M  N  L  U  B  T
```

All these words are found in *Call It Courage*. Using the book and other sources, research the definition of each word. Next write the word and the definition. Then write a sentence using the word. Use the back of the page to complete all fifteen words. A sample is provided.

Word: _puaa_

Definition: _a wild pig_

Sentence: _I ran away from a puaa._

CALL IT COURAGE

Directions

Everybody has been afraid at some time. Whether based on fact or fantasy, fear is a natural human emotion. for some, it is more intense than for others. Some common fears are fear of snakes, storms, dark, fire, heights, and losing a loved one. In the spaces below, complete the statements.

ACTIVITY SHEET 2

My greatest fear is _____

I have shared my fear with _____

I believe I have this fear because _____

_____

_____

I have tried to overcome my fear by _____

_____

_____

To understand a fear and then overcome it is an act of courage exhibited by Mafatu in *Call It Courage*. My plan to overcome my fear is

_____

_____

Create a slogan for a bumper sticker that summarizes how you can rid yourself of your fear. Illustrate your bumper sticker in the space below:

From *Read It Again: Book 2, A Guide for Teaching Reading Through Literature* published by Scott, Foresman and Company. Copyright © 1990 Liz Rothlein and Terri Christman.

CALL IT
COURAGE

Name _____ Date _____

Directions
Courage is an honorable and desirable trait. In the book *Call It Courage*, the island people of Hikueru worship courage; without it, a person is considered a failure. Think about what courage means to you and complete the following:

To me, courage is _____

_____

The dictionary definition of courage is _____

_____

Do you agree that Mafatu exhibits courage in the book? Why or why not?

_____

_____

What person that you know would you consider courageous? _____

What characteristics make this person courageous? _____

_____

Is it possible to have courage in one aspect of life and not in others? _____

Explain: _____

_____

Create a badge in the space below that you feel exemplifies courage:

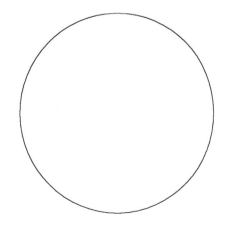

CALL IT COURAGE

Additional Activities

1 Divide your students into groups, and assign each group one of the following research projects. Later allow students time to share their findings.

Group 1: There are many stories about eaters-of-men. Investigate to find out if eaters-of-men actually did exist.

Group 2: What is the island of Hikueru in the South Seas of the Pacific Ocean like today? Describe its people, culture, climate, vegetation, and so on. What would living there be like?

Group 3: Describe the Polynesian people and their culture as it was in the early days compared to the way it is today.

Group 4: Investigate the islands surrounding Hikueru to find out where Mafatu may have sailed. Describe this island as it exists today, and explain why you selected it.

Group 5: Many groups of people have worshiped gods as Mafatu's people do. Select one and describe their gods compared to the gods of Mafatu's people.

Group 6: Mafatu makes many tools, which he needs to exist on the island. Find pictures or descriptions of tools used by the Polynesians of early times. Compare these to today's tools used for similar purposes.

2 Provide students with the opportunity to make a replica of Mafatu's boat as described in the book.

3 Write the saying "It is like an albatross around my neck" on the chalkboard. Tell students to investigate the origin and meaning of this saying and then compare their findings to the role of the albatross in *Call It Courage*.

4 Tell students to find out as much as possible about Polynesian foods. Polynesian restaurants can be found throughout the United States. Perhaps a group of students could locate a Polynesian restaurant and obtain a menu. Also, Polynesian cookbooks are available. After an investigation of Polynesian foods, have students plan a Polynesian tasting party, each contributing in some manner.

5 Mafatu's name means Stout Heart. Ask students to find out, if possible, what their first and last names mean and how they originated. Provide time to share this information with the class.

From *Read It Again: Book 2, A Guide for Teaching Reading Through Literature* published by Scott, Foresman and Company. Copyright © 1990 Liz Rothlein and Terri Christman.

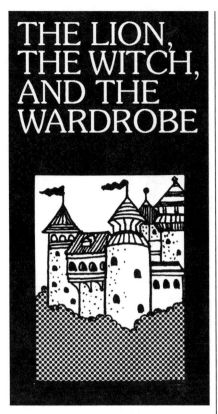

THE LION, THE WITCH, AND THE WARDROBE

Author
C. S. Lewis

Illustrator
Pauline Baynes

Publisher
C. S. Lewis Pte. Ltd., 1950

Pages	Reading Level	Interest Level
186	5	4–6

Other Books by Lewis
Prince Caspian; The Voyage of the "Dawn Treader"; The Silver Chair; The Horse and His Boy; The Magician's Nephew; The Last Battle; The Complete Chronicles of Narnia

From *Read It Again: Book 2, A Guide for Teaching Reading Through Literature* published by Scott, Foresman and Company. Copyright © 1990 Liz Rothlein and Terri Christman.

Information About the Author
C. S. Lewis is a pseudonym used by Clive Hamilton when he wrote books. Mr. Lewis was born on November 29, 1898, in Belfast, Ireland, and died on November 22, 1963, in Oxford, England. He was married but had no children. He was a novelist, scholar, and critic of English literature. He was also a lecturer at many universities. He wrote novels as well as children's books. He won the Lewis Carroll Shelf Award in 1962 for his book *The Lion, the Witch, and the Wardrobe*. Although some people have complained that *The Lion, the Witch, and the Wardrobe* frightens children, Mr. Lewis thought it frightens some adults but few children.

Summary
Four children (Peter, Susan, Edmund, and Lucy) are sent away from London during the war because of the air raids. They go to the country to live in a large house with an old professor. The professor has no wife, just a housekeeper. While there, the children discover that walking through a wardrobe in an empty room leads to the land of Narnia, a magical place where many things happen to them.

Introduction
The title of the story is *The Lion, the Witch, and the Wardrobe*. What could a lion, a witch, and a wardrobe possibly have in common?

Key Vocabulary
trifle	contentment	reign	inquisitive
passage	dreadful	hoax	spiteful
sulking	logic	premises	harbouring
traitor	betray		

Discussion Questions

1   Describe Lucy's first adventure into the wardrobe. (Answers may vary.)

2   Why won't Edmund tell the others that he has gone through the wardrobe and met Lucy in another land? (Answers may vary.)

3   The children decide to tell the professor about Lucy's adventure. What advice does the professor give the children? How does he explain some of the things she talks about? (Answers may vary.)

4   How do all the children end up in the wardrobe at the same time? (Mrs. Macready is taking sightseers through the house, and she has told the children to stay out of her way. So they hide in the wardrobe.)

5   Explain the changes that take place in Narnia as the spell begins to break. (Answers may vary.)

6   Which character would you like to be? Explain. (Answers may vary.)

7   How do King Peter, King Edmund, Queen Susan, and Queen Lucy govern Narnia? (Answers may vary.)

8   Explain the last sentence in the book: "But if the Professor was right it was only the beginning of the adventures of Narnia." (Answers may vary.)

Bulletin Board

In *The Lion, the Witch, and the Wardrobe* the children discover the magical land of Narnia. Talk to students about how Narnia is discovered by accident: The children are all hiding from Mrs. Macready in the wardrobe. All of a sudden, Susan is sitting against a tree, there is snow all around them, and so on. Have students pretend they hid in a wardrobe and found a Narnia. Then ask them to illustrate (on a sheet of 8½ × 11 piece of paper) their Narnia. Now have them color the wardrobe on the next page, cut it out (making sure to cut in the center between the doors), and glue the edges of the wardrobe over their drawing. When they open their wardrobe doors they will see their magical land. Place these projects on the bulletin board, and label it "OUR NARNIA."

From *Read It Again: Book 2, A Guide for Teaching Reading Through Literature* published by Scott, Foresman and Company. Copyright © 1990 Liz Rothlein and Terri Christman.

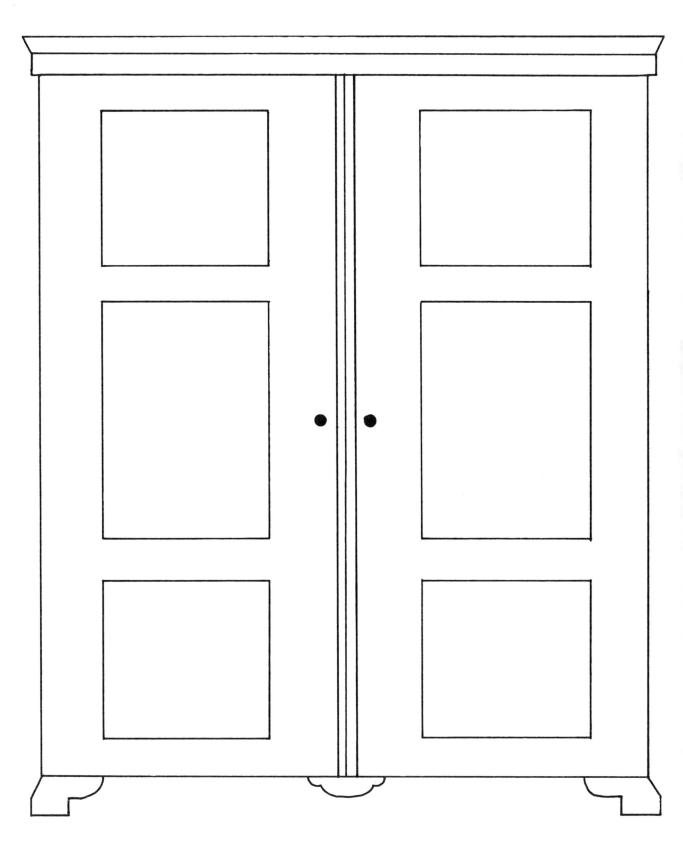

Name _____ Date _____

Directions
On the left-hand side of the page, draw Narnia as it is when the children arrive: cold and snow-covered. On the right-hand side, draw Narnia as it looks when the spell begins to break: flowers, singing birds, blue sky, running water. Next, in paragraph form, write a description for each illustration.

Narnia before	Narnia after
_____	_____
_____	_____
_____	_____
_____	_____
_____	_____
_____	_____

From *Read It Again: Book 2, A Guide for Teaching Reading Through Literature* published by Scott, Foresman and Company. Copyright © 1990 Liz Rothlein and Terri Christman.

From *Read It Again! Book 2, A Guide for Teaching Reading Through Literature* published by Scott, Foresman and Company. Copyright © 1990 Liz Rothlein and Terri Christman.

THE LION, THE WITCH, AND THE WARDROBE

ACTIVITY SHEET 2

Name _____ Date _____

Directions

Some things in *The Lion, the Witch, and the Wardrobe* could happen in real life (reality). Some things could not happen in real life (fantasy). Read the sentences below. Circle the correct word for each sentence.

reality   fantasy   a. All four children walk through the wardrobe into Narnia

reality   fantasy   b. Mrs. Beaver is busily working at her sewing machine.

reality   fantasy   c. The children are playing hide-and-seek.

reality   fantasy   d. Lucy and the Faun meet.

reality   fantasy   e. The children are hiding from Mrs. Macready.

reality   fantasy   f. The Queen gives Edmund Turkish Delight.

reality   fantasy   g. Aslan does not die because of the Deep Magic.

reality   fantasy   h. They rescue the Faun from the Witch's fortress.

reality   fantasy   i. The children are sent to live with an old professor.

reality   fantasy   j. Mrs. Macready is taking a party of sightseers through the house.

Next, sequence the ten sentences from above in the order in which they happen in the story. The first one is done for you.

1. _*i*_   2. _____   3. _____   4. _____   5. _____

6. _____   7. _____   8. _____   9. _____ 10. _____

THE LION,
THE WITCH,
AND THE
WARDROBE

**ACTIVITY
SHEET 3**

Name _____ Date _____

Directions

On the lines accompanying each drawing, write words that best describe the person, place, or thing. Cut out one of these and glue it on a piece of writing paper. In paragraph form, use the descriptive words to describe it.

The
Witch

_____

_____

Aslan _____

_____

_____

From *Read It Again: Book 2, A Guide for Teaching Reading Through Literature* published by Scott, Foresman and Company. Copyright © 1990 Liz Rothlein and Terri Christman.

Lucy _____

_____

_____

Narnia _____

_____

Additional Activities

1 Discuss with the students how Narnia was experiencing only winter because of the witch's spell. Talk about the other three seasons—spring, summer, and fall. Have students pretend that where they live they can have only one season forever. Have them select the one season they would like to have and, orally or in writing, explain why they selected that season. Share the responses with the class. Create a graph on the chalkboard to see which season was chosen the most frequently, the least frequently, and so on.

2 C. S. Lewis has written many other stories about Narnia: *Prince Caspian; The Voyage of the "Dawn Treader"; The Silver Chair; The Horse and His Boy; The Magician's Nephew; The Complete Chronicles of Narnia;* and *The Last Battle.* Choose one or more of these books to share aloud with students. Have students compare the books. Discuss which one they like best and least.

3 Discuss the many interesting characters in *The Lion, the Witch, and the Wardrobe.* They include Lucy, Edmund, Peter, Susan, the Professor, Mrs. Macready, the Faun (Mr. Tumnus), Mr. and Mrs. Beaver, the White Witch, Aslan, dryads, naiads, dwarfs, the grey wolf, Father Christmas, giants, ghouls, boggles, ogres, minotaurs, cruels, hags, spectres, the people of toadstools, centaurs, unicorns, incubuses, wraiths, horrors, efreets, sprites, orknies, wooses, ettins, and Giant Rumblebuffin. Some of the characters are described well, some are not. Have students create one of the characters by drawing, coloring, and cutting it out. Be sure each character is labeled. Place all the characters on a bulletin board, chalkboard, or large piece of cardboard to create a collage of the land of Narnia.

4 In this story, Edmund describes the White Witch as a great lady, taller than any woman he has ever seen. She is covered in white fur up to her throat, wears a golden crown, and holds a long, straight golden wand in her right hand. Her face is white—like snow or paper or sugar icing—except for her very red mouth. It is a beautiful face but proud and cold and stern. Give students white yarn, white construction paper, and white fur to create the White Witch. Have them place their creations on black construction paper. Then, have them describe her appearance in paragraph form in their own words.

5 In this story, students see Lucy, Edmund, Peter, and Susan change. Have students fold a piece of paper in half. They should label the left-hand side of the paper "The Beginning" and the right-hand side of the paper "The End." Then they should list each child's name on both sides of the paper. Have them give a brief description of each character—how he or she is in the beginning of the story and at the end of the story. Remember, the children become kings and queens.

6 Reread the author information, pointing out that C. S. Lewis is a pseudonym, not a real name. Discuss with students what other authors they know have pseudonyms and why an author would choose to have one.

From *Read It Again: Book 2, A Guide for Teaching Reading Through Literature* published by Scott, Foresman and Company. Copyright © 1990 Liz Rothlein and Terri Christman.

LITTLE HOUSE IN THE BIG WOODS

Author
Laura Ingalls Wilder

Illustrator
Garth Williams

Publisher
Harper & Row, 1932

Pages 238	Reading Level 5	Interest Level 4–6

Other Books by Wilder
Little House on the Prairie; Farmer Boy; On the Banks of Plum Creek; By the Shores of Silver Lake; The Long Winter; The First Four Years; Little Town on the Prairie; These Happy Golden Years

Information About the Author

Laura Ingalls was born in 1867 in a little log cabin on the edge of the Big Woods in Wisconsin. While she was growing up, she traveled with her family in a covered wagon through Kansas, Minnesota, and finally the Dakota Territory, where she met and married Almanzo Wilder. She lived a pioneer life filled with deprivation and hard work, but there were also good times filled with laughter and love. *Little House in the Big Woods* was the first of a series of nine autobiographical books that Mrs. Wilder wrote. She once said that she lived everything that happened in the books she wrote. A Laura Ingalls Wilder Medal was established by the American Library Association to honor authors and illustrators who contribute over a period of time to children's literature. Mrs. Wilder died in 1957 at the age of ninety.

Summary

This is a true story about Laura Ingalls Wilder and her family during the 1870s. They live in a log cabin deep in the Wisconsin woods, where wolves, panthers, and bears roam. Pa Ingalls hunts, traps, and farms to provide for his wife and three daughters—Mary, Laura, and Baby Carrie. Ma Ingalls cooks, sews, and cleans. This book is simply written with vivid details that provide an account of Laura's frontier life as a child.

Introduction

This is a true story about Laura Ingalls Wilder. She lives in a log cabin deep in the Wisconsin woods, where wolves, panthers, and bears roam. The book is also about love and laughter as the family shares in holiday celebrations, sleigh rides, and socials. What are your earliest memories of your childhood?

Key Vocabulary

brindle	ravines	solemn
roamed	curlicues	swagger
kerosene	hearth	trundle bed

LITTLE HOUSE IN THE BIG WOODS

Discussion Questions

1   When and where does the story take place? (It takes place in the 1870s in Wisconsin.)

2   What do you think you would like best about living in the 1870s? What do you think you would like least about living in the 1870s? Explain. (Answers may vary.)

3   Laura and her family eat many different kinds of food. Name four different ones and tell how the Ingalls get those foods. (Answers may vary but may include deer (venison), which the father hunts; butter, which the mother churns from milk; headcheese, which is made from the head of a hog they butcher.)

4   On Christmas, who comes to visit the Ingalls family? How do they come? (Laura's aunt, uncle, and cousins arrive by bobsled.)

5   In this story, the boys and men have different responsibilities from the girls and women. What are some of the responsibilities of boys and men? What are some of the responsibilities of girls and women? (Boys and men hunt, trap, build, butcher, and the like; girls and women do things like make butter and sugar, sew, clean, care for the children, cook, and bake.) Has this definition of roles changed since the time of the book? Explain. What is your opinion of male and female roles today? (Answers may vary.)

6   How do you think Laura feels about her sister Mary? Explain and give examples from the story. (Answers may vary.)

7   Why do you think Uncle Henry allows Charley to behave the way he does when they harvest the oats? (Answers may vary.)

8   The Ingalls live in a log cabin in Wisconsin. Compare the log cabin with your home. What are the similarities and differences? (Answers may vary.)

Bulletin Board

Ask students to find out from their parents, grandparents, aunts, and uncles about quilts the family may have. Allow them to share these real quilts or pictures of quilts with the class. Obtain quilting books, such as *The Quilt Story* by Tony Johnson or *The Quilt* by Ann Jonas, and allow students time to read the books. Then provide students with various colors of construction paper cut into 8-inch squares. Ask each student to make a design on a square. When all squares are completed, arrange them on the bulletin board to resemble a real quilt. Put the caption "OUR CLASS QUILT" on the bulletin board. Note: Students could also use squares of fabric and actually make a quilt.

From *Read It Again!: Book 2, A Guide for Teaching Reading Through Literature* published by Scott, Foresman and Company. Copyright © 1990 Liz Rothlein and Terri Christman.

LITTLE HOUSE
IN THE BIG
WOODS

**ACTIVITY
SHEET 1**

From *Read It Again: Book 2, A Guide for Teaching Reading Through Literature* published by Scott, Foresman and Company. Copyright © 1990 Liz Rothlein and Terri Christman.

Name _____ Date _____

Directions

Match the characters' names with their descriptions by putting the correct letter of the description in the blank in front of the character's name.

Characters	**Descriptions**
____ 1. Ma Ingalls	a. doll made from rags
____ 2. Pa Ingalls	b. comes in and out, day or night, as she pleases
____ 3. Laura Ingalls	c. helps Pa Ingalls butcher the pig
____ 4. Mary Ingalls	d. makes headcheese from the pig's head
____ 5. George	e. doll made from a corncob wrapped in a handkerchief
____ 6. Jack	f. person Pa Ingalls refers to as "my little half-pint of sweet cider half drunk up"
____ 7. Uncle Henry	g. tears off a piece of Aunt Eliza's skirt trying to save her
____ 8. Nettie	h. cousin who visits at Christmas and wants to make pictures in the snow
____ 9. Susan	i. tells jokes and riddles and plays a fiddle
____ 10. Prince	j. helps guard the Ingalls' home
____ 11. Black Susan	k. would have been eaten by a bear if the dog hadn't interfered
____ 12. Aunt Eliza	l. sister with beautiful blond curls
____ 13. Carrie	m. baby of the Ingalls family
____ 14. Alice	n. uncle that pa says is wild
____ 15. Charley	o. cousin who misbehaves in the fields

Which of the above characters best fits the life of a pioneer? _____

Why? _____

_____

Which of the above characters least fits the life of a pioneer? _____

Why? _____

_____

**ACTIVITY
SHEET 2**

Directions
Many events take place in this story. Select the six that you
feel are most significant and list them below in the order
they happen.

Event 1 _____

_____

Event 2 _____

_____

Event 3 _____

_____

Event 4 _____

_____

Event 5 _____

_____

Event 6 _____

_____

Of these events,* which do you think is the

happiest _____ most believable _____

saddest _____ least believable _____

funniest _____ most informative _____

Which of these events would you like to have been involved in? _____

_____

*If none of the events you have selected apply, put NA for not applicable.

From *Read It Again: Book 2, A Guide for Teaching Reading Through Literature* published by Scott, Foresman and Company. Copyright © 1990 Liz Rothlein and Terri Christman.

Name _____ Date _____

**ACTIVITY
SHEET 3**

Directions

Webbing, or semantic mapping, is a way of organizing or outlining information about a topic. Try webbing or semantic mapping the words "pioneer life" as experienced by the Ingalls family. To do so, you need to think of other key words associated with "pioneer days," then other words associated with the key words, and so forth. The example given for the word "curious" may be of help.

Example

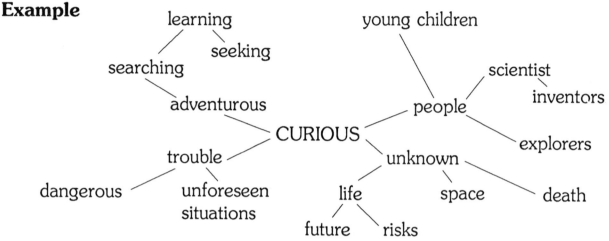

PIONEER LIFE

Choose a tune that you know. Then, using the words generated in the mapping exercise, write new lyrics about pioneer life to accompany the tune, so Pa Ingalls can play it in the evenings on his fiddle. You may want to ask a friend or music teacher to help you with the melody. Use the other side of this paper.

LITTLE HOUSE IN THE BIG WOODS

Additional Activities

1 Locate Wisconsin on a United States map; then locate your state. Discuss with the class how the two states are similar and how they are different—for example, weather, terrain, food, and animal products. Ask students to pretend they are going to drive to Wisconsin. Obtain road maps and plan the best route.

2 Provide students with dictionaries, encyclopedias, and other appropriate reference materials. Ask them to research the following list of words and phrases:

chopping block	keg of nails	trundle bed	grubbing hoe
butter churn	wagon box	samplers	pokeberries
nine-patch quilt	traplines	yokes	trough
corset			

Once these words have been researched, encourage students to make a display of as many of the items as possible, using either real objects or pictures to represent the words. As a culminating activity, make a class picture dictionary of these terms.

3 Laura and the other children in this book play many games. Ask students to tell you all the games, activities, and play materials mentioned in *Little House in the Big Woods* as you write the list on the chalkboard. Then ask students to tell you which items on the list would most likely be mentioned in modern times. Mark these on the chalkboard. Next, make a list of games popular today, and mark the ones that might have been played in the 1870s. Finally, examine the two lists and determine which activities that were popular in the 1870s are still popular today. Make a third list of those games activities and play materials.

Played in the 1870s	**Played Today**	**Played in the 1870s and Today**
ball with balloon made from pig's bladder	video games	dolls

4 Ask students to collect enough small jars with lids so that each person has a jar (baby food jars work well). In each jar, pour ¼ cup of cream. If possible, put a marble in each jar to aid mixing. Instruct students to shake each jar until butter forms. Pour off the remaining liquid (the whey) into a larger jar. Provide students with bread or crackers on which to spread the butter. Salt can be added to enhance the flavor. Remind students that this process of making butter is similar to using a butter churn.

5 Make available the other eight books by Laura Ingalls Wilder, which trace her life from the days in the Big Woods to the 1880s, when she was married and homesteading in the Dakotas and gave birth to her daughter, Rose. As a culminating activity, trace on a map the travels of the Ingalls family from Pepin, Wisconsin, to DeSmet, South Dakota, to Walnut Grove, Minnesota, to Burr Oak, Iowa, back to Walnut Grove, back to DeSmet, and finally to Mansfield, Missouri. Students may want to calculate the miles

From *Read It Again: Book 2, A Guide for Teaching Reading Through Literature* published by Scott, Foresman and Company. Copyright © 1990 Liz Rothlein and Terri Christman.

LITTLE HOUSE IN THE BIG WOODS

traveled and the time the trip may have taken by different forms of transportation (such as plane, train, car, stagecoach, wagon, foot, buggy).

6 Find tapes, song books, and records to demonstrate the songs that Pa plays on his fiddle: "Auld Lang Syne," "Pop Goes the Weasel," "Home, Sweet Home," and so on. Teach students the words and music for these songs.

7 Teach students some simple square dances. Square dance records with directions can be purchased or perhaps borrowed from the physical education teacher or the music teacher.

8 Organize a guessing game about characters in *Little House in the Big Woods* by writing the following open-ended clues on the chalkboard. Then tell students to privately choose one of the characters in the book and to secretly complete each of the following statements:

Clue 1: In the book my character said _____

Clue 2: I would best describe my character's looks as _____

Clue 3: Something my character did was _____

Clue 4: My character was important in the story because _____

Once all the students have compiled their clues, allow one student to give Clue 1. The other students then get two chances to guess the character. If nobody guesses correctly, proceed to Clue 2 and allow two more guesses. Continue with the clues until the character is guessed. The person who guesses the character is next for giving clues.

THE SECRET GARDEN

Author
Frances Hodgson Burnett

Illustrator
Tasha Tudor

Publisher
Harper & Row, 1962

Pages 311	Reading Level 5	Interest Level 3–5

Other Books by Burnett
Sara Crewe; A Little Princess; The Lost Prince; Little Lord Fauntleroy

Information About the Author
Frances Hodgson Burnett was born on November 24, 1849, in Manchester, England. She came to the United States in 1865 and made her home in Long Island, New York. She began writing for publication at the age of seventeen as a novelist and children's writer. She loved working with her hands—digging, pulling weeds, and the like. She wrote about the gardens of her childhood years in Islington, England. Many of the gardens there were not taken care of and were locked. One of her best-known books, *The Secret Garden*, was written about such a place. She died on October 29, 1924, in Long Island, New York.

Summary
When Mary Lennox, an orphaned, lonely, sickly, and contrary little girl, comes to live at her uncle's big manor house on the wind-swept Yorkshire moors, she finds that it is full of secrets. As she wanders about, she discovers a locked and abandoned garden and her uncle's invalid child, Colin. He and Dickon, a magical boy from the countryside who charms wild animals, become Mary's first friends and help her discover herself.

Introduction
Mary, a lonely, orphaned, and contrary nine-year-old girl, finds herself in a big manor house on the English moors, living with an uncle who doesn't care about her. She has never had a friend or anyone who loves her. Read the story to find out how she feels when she meets Dickon, a boy from the countryside who becomes her friend and confidant, as well as Colin, her sickly cousin who comes to rely on her.

Key Vocabulary
cholera	appalling	disagreeable	moor
brougham	obstinate	contrary	subservient
impudent			

From *Read It Again: Book 2, A Guide for Teaching Reading Through Literature* published by Scott, Foresman and Company. Copyright © 1990 Liz Rothlein and Terri Christman.

THE SECRET GARDEN

Discussion Questions

1 Where is Mary first taken after her parents' death? (She is taken to an English clergyman's home.)

2 What nickname does the clergyman's son give Mary? (He calls her Mistress Mary Quite Contrary.)

3 Where is Mary taken after she leaves the clergyman's home? (She goes to London and then to Misselthwaite Manor on the Yorkshire moors.)

4 How might Mary's life be different if her parents had not died of cholera? (Answers may vary.)

5 At what point in the story does Mary begin to be less contrary and selfish and begin to be a more normal, caring little girl? (Answers may vary.)

6 Does Mary do the right thing to Colin the night he has hysterics? Why or why not? (Answers may vary.)

7 Explain what is meant in this story by the quote "When you tend a rose, my lad, a thistle cannot grow." (Answers may vary.)

8 In what period of time does this story take place? Explain. (Answers may vary.)

Bulletin Board

In large letters, put the caption "THE SECRET GARDEN" on the bulletin board. Ask students and their parents to help you collect brochures and magazines with many pictures of flowers, trees, shrubs, and birds. As a group, plan a bulletin board garden that best depicts Mary, Dickon, and Colin's secret garden. Include paths, walls, and plants.

THE SECRET
GARDEN

**ACTIVITY
SHEET 1**

Directions
Complete the following:

In *The Secret Garden*, Colin refers to changes and happenings as "The Magic."
Briefly explain what he means by "The Magic":

_____

_____

_____

Describe the magic you would select for yourself: _____

_____

_____

Explain your choice: _____

_____

Identify a friend or relative and describe the kind of magic you would select for
him or her:

Name of relative/friend: _____

"The Magic" selected: _____

_____

Explain your choice: _____

_____

Finally, do you believe that magic exists as described in the book?

_____

_____

Why or why not? _____

_____

From *Read It Again: Book 2, A Guide for Teaching Reading Through Literature* published by Scott, Foresman and Company. Copyright © 1990 Liz Rothlein and Terri Christman.

Name _____ Date _____

Directions

Pretend that Mary moves from India to live in your neighborhood. Read each of the situations below, and then answer the questions based on how you feel about each situation after reading the story.

Situation 1 Mary has just arrived from India and has moved in with your closest neighbor, whom you like very much. Mary is selfish, ugly, and contrary. Your neighbor comes over and asks you to take Mary to school with you and to introduce her to all your friends. How do you think you would react? Why?

_____

_____

_____

Situation 2 Your best friend tells you about Mary, a new, strange girl from India. Your friend tells you that Mary is a nasty, ugly little girl that no one would want to be with. Yet when you meet Mary, she tells you about a secret hiding place she has found and invites you to join her. What would you do? Explain.

_____

_____

_____

Situation 3 Suppose Mary is your cousin and has just moved from India to live with you and your family because her parents have died. Given what you already know about how Mary behaved at the time of her parents' death, what advice would you give her to help her adjust to her new home?

_____

_____

_____

_____

THE SECRET
GARDEN

**ACTIVITY
SHEET 3**

Name _____ Date _____

Directions

The sentences below are from *The Secret Garden*. Rewrite these sentences using different words for the ones underlined but still keeping the meaning. A dictionary or thesaurus may help you.

1. She had not wanted a little girl at all, and when Mary was born she handed her over to the care of an <u>Ayah</u> _____, who was made to understand that if she wished to please the Mem Sahib she must keep the child out of sight as much as possible.

2. "What <u>desolation</u> _____!" she heard one voice say.

3. Then they had passed a church and a <u>vicarage</u> _____ and a little shop window or so in a cottage with toys and sweets and odd things set out for sale.

4. She was <u>imperious</u> _____ and Indian, and at the same time hot and sorrowful.

5. He open his eyes quite wide with <u>indignation</u> _____.

6. "Shall we sway backward and forward, Mary, as if we were <u>dervishes</u> _____?"

7. Mistress Mary felt solemnly <u>enraptured</u> _____.

8. "Tell her she has been most <u>bounteous</u> _____ and our gratitude is extreme."

9. After the morning's <u>incantations</u> _____ Colin sometimes gave them Magic Lectures.

10. They were <u>obsequious</u> _____ and <u>servile</u> _____ and did not presume to talk to their masters as if they were equals.

11. "Once in India I saw a boy was a <u>Rajah</u> _____."

12. "I knew he'd come," said Martha <u>exultantly</u> _____.

THE SECRET GARDEN

Additional Activities

1 In this story, Mary is nicknamed "Mistress Mary Quite Contrary," and the children dance around her and sing the following nursery rhyme:

> Mistress Mary, quite contrary,
> How does your garden grow?
> With silver bells, and cockel shells,
> And marigolds all in a row.

Ask a group of students to investigate the origin of this nursery rhyme to determine if it originated before, after, or as a result of the book *The Secret Garden*.

Next, provide students with a variety of nursery rhyme books, such as *Marguerite de Angeli's Book of Nursery and Mother Goose Rhymes*, Iona and Peter Opie's *The Oxford Nursery Rhyme Book*, and Arthur Rackham's *Mother Goose: The Old Nursery Rhymes*. Allow time for students to select other nursery rhymes about people, such as "Peter, Peter, Pumpkin Eater," "Old King Cole," and "Little Miss Muffet." Write the titles on the chalkboard.

Then divide the class into groups of four or five students. Assign each group nursery rhymes different from those listed on the chalkboard. Tell each group to create a short story in which the nursery rhyme character is integrated into the story, as Mistress Mary was integrated into *The Secret Garden*.

2 If possible, obtain a small piece of ground on the school premises where students can have a garden. If no space is available, consider a window sill garden. Before planting the garden, investigate what will grow and what will not grow there. Invite a gardener or horticulturist into your classroom to discuss gardening. Consider planting some seeds similar to those Mary plants in the secret garden.

3 Using sources such as an encyclopedia, help your students understand more about what an English moor is like. If possible, invite someone from England into your class to talk about moors. Finally, develop a class mural depicting a moor or simulate a moor by using sand, clay, sticks, grass, and other natural materials.

4 On a world map, locate India and England. Using yarn or string and thumbtacks or tape, stretch a string from one point to the other. Discuss with students the route of the train voyage that Mary and Mrs. Medlock take.

5 Provide students with books about India and England. Tell them to investigate the two countries and compare their customs, government, climate, population, and other features.

6 The story *The Secret Garden* is available as a movie as well as on record or cassette. The movie was made in 1949 by Loew's and starred Margaret O'Brien. The record/cassette of the story, read by Claire Bloom, is available from Caedmon or, read by Glenda Jackson, from Miller-Brody Products. Allow students time to listen or watch any of these presentations and then compare it with the book form. Discuss which students like best and why.

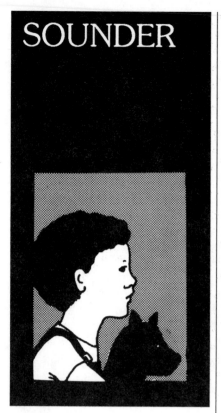

SOUNDER

Author
William H. Armstrong

Illustrator
James Barkley

Publisher
Harper & Row, 1969

Pages 116	Reading Level 5	Interest Level 4–6

Other Books by Armstrong
My Animals; Animal Tales; Hadassah; Esther, the Orphan Queen

Information About the Author

William Armstrong was born on September 14, 1914, in Lexington, Virginia. He was married and had three children. As an adult, he lived in a house that he built on Kimadee Hill in Kent, Connecticut, where he raised sheep and was an author. There he wrote *Sounder*, a Newbery Medal award winner that has been translated into eight languages and was made into a film by Twentieth Century Fox in 1972. The story came from memories of stories he had heard many years before from a black man. Mr. Armstrong wrote the book during the early part of the winter, and it remained on a shelf until the day Mr. Armstrong asked a neighbor to read it. The neighbor liked it. William Armstrong died in 1953 at the age of 39.

Summary

Sounder is a compelling story of a boy's tenacity for life in a black sharecropper's family. It is a story of courage, human dignity, and love.

Introduction

This is a story about a black sharecropper's family and their dog, Sounder. In this story, a young boy faces many hardships. He never has the opportunity to be a child. Instead, because of a tragedy that befalls his father, he has to assume the responsibilities of an adult. As you read the story, think how you would react if you were thrown into a similar situation.

Key Vocabulary

cabin	possum	preacher	sharecropper
foothills	kernels	straw tick	quarry

SOUNDER

From *Read It Again: Book 2, A Guide for Teaching Reading Through Literature* published by Scott, Foresman and Company. Copyright © 1990 Liz Rothlein and Terri Christman.

Discussion Questions

1 Why do the men take the father off to jail? (They take him because he stole the ham.)

2 Why does the mother hum while she cooks the ham in the morning before the father is taken off to jail? (Answers may vary but might include because she knows the ham is stolen and is worried.)

3 What happens to the father in jail that makes him a cripple? (After a dynamite blast in one of the prison quarries, he is crushed under an avalanche of limestone.)

4 Why does Sounder never make any of his usual loud sounds until he sees the father coming down the road? (Answers may vary but might include because he missed his master.)

5 How did you feel at the end of the story? What happens in the story that made you feel this way? (Answers may vary.)

6 In what period of history do you think this story takes place? Why? Give approximate dates and backup information from the story that reinforce your estimate. (Answers may vary.)

7 Are there families in the United States with lifestyles similar to that of the boy's family? If so, give examples. (Answers may vary.)

8 Describe what you think the boy's adult life may be like. (Answers may vary.)

Bulletin Board
Using large letters, put the caption "THE GREATEST DOG ON EARTH" on the bulletin board. Then ask students to provide a written description and a picture of their idea of "the greatest dog on earth." Allow time for students to explain why their dog is the greatest dog.

SOUNDER | Name _____ Date _____

Directions
If the boy had been able to write a letter to his father while his father was in jail, what do you think the boy would have said? Write such a letter to the father.

(Date) _____

(Greeting) Dear Father,

_____

_____

_____

_____

_____

_____

(Body) _____

_____

_____

_____

_____

_____

(Closing) With love,

(Signature)

From *Read It Again: Book 2, A Guide for Teaching Reading Through Literature* published by Scott, Foresman and Company. Copyright © 1990 Liz Rothlein and Terri Christman.

SOUNDER | Name _____ Date _____

ACTIVITY SHEET 2

Directions

People have traits that are considered good and traits that are considered bad. Make a list of traits that you would consider good—for example, honest and caring—and a list of traits that you would consider bad—for example, deceitful and cruel.

Good Traits   Bad Traits

_____   _____

_____   _____

_____   _____

Name three characters from the story who have good traits and three characters with bad traits. In addition, list the most significant good or bad trait for each.

Characters with Good Traits   Most Significant Good Trait

1._____   _____

2._____   _____

3._____   _____

Characters with Bad Traits   Most Significant Bad Trait

1._____   _____

2._____   _____

3._____   _____

Directions

Name three of your best friends, and identify one good or bad trait for each. Circle the appropriate word to indicate whether you think the trait is good or bad.

Name of Friend   Trait

1._____   _____ Good Bad

2._____   _____ Good Bad

3._____   _____ Good Bad

SOUNDER | Name ——————————————— Date ————————

ACTIVITY
SHEET 3

Directions
At the beginning of *Sounder*, there is the following quote on courage by Antoine de Saint Exupery: "A man keeps, like his love, his courage dark." Explain how you think this quotation relates to the book.

_____

_____

_____

_____

Using *Bartlett's Book of Familiar Quotations*, find three other quotations on courage and write them in the space provided.

_____

_____

_____

_____

_____

Create your own quotation on courage.

_____

_____

Select the character from the book who you feel had the most courage. Defend your selection.

Name of character: _____

Defense of your selection: _____

_____

_____

From *Read It Again: Book 2, A Guide for Teaching Reading Through Literature* published by Scott, Foresman and Company. Copyright © 1990 Liz Rothlein and Terri Christman.

SOUNDER

Additional Activities

1 In the author's note at the beginning of the book, W. H. Armstrong discusses the origin of the story. Ask students to reread the author's note, and then ask them if they believe *Sounder* is a true story or a make-believe story. On the chalkboard, list examples to reinforce each position.

2 Tell students to use an encyclopedia and other appropriate sources to research the coon dog, the type of dog Sounder is. Tell them to find out about the dog's size, what it likes to eat, and other characteristics peculiar to the coon dog. When their research is complete, provide time for the students to compare what they found out with what is written about Sounder and decide if Sounder was a typical coon dog.

3 Remind students that the family in *Sounder* is a sharecropper family. Provide time for students to investigate the meaning of being a sharecropper and finally write a definition. Following this exercise, ask each student to find at least one book that relates to sharecroppers, read the book, and then write the bibliographic information and a brief summary on a 3×5 card. Finally, compile a class file of these cards. This activity will provide students with not only a better understanding of sharecroppers but also an understanding of what an annotated bibliography is.

4 If possible, invite a judge or attorney into the classroom to discuss what the legal procedures would be today if someone was caught stealing a ham. Tell the guest what happens to the father in *Sounder* when he is caught stealing the ham. Debate the pros and cons of such punishment. Perhaps you can set up a mock trial depicting this situation.

5 Some people believe in superstitions, such as breaking a mirror brings seven years of bad luck. In *Sounder*, the boy is told that putting something under your pillow when you go to bed and making a wish will make the wish come true. After the boy found the ear that had been shot off Sounder, he put it under his pillow and wished that Sounder wasn't dead. Ask students to get examples of superstitions from their family, friends, and neighbors. Make a list of all the superstitions the students have collected. Allow time for them to find the origin of as many of the superstitions as possible. Share these with the class.

APPENDIX

GENERAL ACTIVITY 1

Directions
Do the crossword puzzle by completing the sentences below.

Across

1. Jemmy gets punished for things Prince _____ does.
3. Mafatu goes out into the sea to find _____.
4. The reluctant dragon is covered with blue _____.
6. Sounder's master is put in jail for stealing a _____.
8. The little house in the Big Woods is in _____.
11. The giving tree gives the boy its _____.
12. Mary Lennox's cousin's name is _____.
15. Mr. _____ is a faun that Lucy meets in the land of Narnia.

Down

2. A word Charlotte spins in her web is _____.
5. Sarah misses the _____.
7. Jess and Leslie create Terabithia, a _____ kingdom.
9. Mary Lennox's uncle lives in the _____ of England.
10. Pa Ingalls likes to play the _____.
12. Henry gets a fever because he eats too much _____.
14. Ramona does not think she is a _____.
16. James, orphaned, is sent to live with his mean _____.

From *Read It Again: Book 2, A Guide for Teaching Reading Through Literature* published by Scott, Foresman and Company. Copyright © 1990 Liz Rothlein and Terri Christman.

Name _____ Date _____

GENERAL ACTIVITY 2

Directions
Below is a list of some of the main characters and titles of the books you have read. Mark the face to express how you feel about each.

1. Laura Ingalls (*Little House in the Big Woods*)

2. Wanda Petronski (*The Hundred Dresses*)

3. Henry Green (*Chocolate Fever*)

4. Jess Aarons (*Bridge to Terabithia*)

5. Fern (*Charlotte's Web*)

6. Mafatu (*Call It Courage*)

7. Sarah (*Sarah, Plain and Tall*)

8. Lucy (*The Lion, the Witch, and the Wardrobe*)

9. Jemmy (*The Whipping Boy*)

10. Mary Lennox (*The Secret Garden*)

11. Ramona (*Ramona the Pest*)

12. James (*James and the Giant Peach*)

Which character is your favorite? _____

Explain. _____

Which character is your least favorite? _____

Explain. _____

Which character is most like you? _____

Explain. _____

Directions

Below are the names of books and the names of characters from the books. Match the character with the correct book by putting the letter for the character in the blank.

a. Caleb
b. Mafatu
c. Laura Ingalls

d. Jess Aarons
e. Mary
f. Jemmy

g. Wanda Petronski
h. Templeton
i. Henry

Chocolate
Fever

_____

The
Whipping
Boy

_____

The
Hundred
Dresses

_____

The Secret
Garden

_____

Charlotte's
Web

_____

Call It
Courage

_____

Litle House
in the Big
Woods

_____

Sarah, Plain
and Tall

_____

Bridge to
Terabithia

_____

From *Read It Again: Book 2, A Guide for Teaching Reading Through Literature* published by Scott, Foresman and Company. Copyright © 1990 Liz Rothlein and Terri Christman.

Name _____ Date _____

Directions
Select the character, from one of the fifteen books listed below, that you enjoyed the most or feel you know the best. Use the form that follows to create a bio-poem about the character you have chosen.

The Giving Tree
The Whipping Boy
Chocolate Fever
Sarah, Plain and Tall
The Reluctant Dragon
Charlotte's Web
The Hundred Dresses
The Lion, the Witch, and the Wardrobe

The Bridge to Terabithia
Ramona the Pest
James and the Giant Peach
The Secret Garden
Call It Courage
Sounder
Little House in the Big Woods

Line 1: (first name) _____

Line 2: (title) _____

Line 3: (four words that describe the person) _____ , _____ ,

_____ , and _____ .

Line 4: Lover of (three or more things or ideas) _____ ,

_____ , and _____ .

Line 5: Who believed (one or more ideas) _____

_____ .

Line 6: Who wanted (three things) _____ , _____ ,

and _____ .

Line 7: Who used (three things or methods) _____ ,

_____ , and _____ .

Line 8: Who gave (three things) _____ , _____ ,

and _____ .

Line 9: Who said (a quote) "_____."

Line 10: (last name) _____

Name_____ Date _____

Directions
After you have read *Little House in the Big Woods, Sarah, Plain and Tall, The Secret Garden, and Sounder,* illustrate the setting of each book in the boxes.

Little House in the Big Woods	*Sarah, Plain and Tall*
The Secret Garden	*Sounder*

How are these settings similar? _____

_____

How are these settings different? _____

_____

Which setting did you like best? _____

Why?_____

_____

Name _____ Date _____

Directions

Read the book titles below and select five that you would like to change. Create a new title for each book, and then tell why you chose that title.

GENERAL ACTIVITY 6

The Giving Tree
Sarah, Plain and Tall
Charlotte's Web
Bridge to Terabithia
James and the Giant Peach
Call it Courage
Chocolate Fever
The Lion, the Witch, and the Wardrobe

The Whipping Boy
The Reluctant Dragon
The Hundred Dresses
Ramona the Pest
The Secret Garden
Sounder
Little House in the Big Woods

1. I would change the title of _____

    to _____

    because _____

2. I would change the title of _____

    to _____

    because _____

3. I would change the title of _____

    to _____

    because _____

4. I would change the title of _____

    to _____

    because _____

5. I would change the title of _____

    to _____

    because _____

Name _____ Date _____

Directions

Select an author you would like to know more about. If the author is still living, write him or her a letter asking for specific information. If this is not possible, visit the library and consult *Something About the Author: Facts and Pictures About Authors and Illustrators of Books for Young Children*, which is an ongoing reference series. Authors' addresses can often be found in this book, or letters can be sent to the author via the publisher. Another reference source is *Yesterday's Authors for Children*, which is a two-volume set focusing on early authors and illustrators (from the beginnings of children's literature through 1960) whose books are being read by children today.

Once you have obtained information about the author, complete the following:

GENERAL ACTIVITY 7

1. Name of author: _____

   Is this the author's real name or a pseudonym (a name that is made up)?

   _____

   If the name is a pseudonym, what is the author's real name?

   _____

2. How many books has the author written for children? _____

3. What is your favorite book that this author has written? _____

   _____

4. Why does the author write books for children? _____

   _____

5. Where does the author get his or her ideas for writing books? _____

   _____

6. What career(s), if any, has the author had besides writing? _____

   _____

7. What additional information did you find out about the author you researched?

   _____

106 READ IT AGAIN! BOOK 2

From *Read It Again: Book 2, A Guide for Teaching Reading Through Literature* published by Scott, Foresman and Company. Copyright © 1990 Liz Rothlein and Terri Christman.

Name _____ Date _____

Directions

A fact is something that can be proven as true. For example, "Airplanes can fly" is a fact. An opinion is something that cannot be proven true. For example, "Flying is fun" is an opinion. Read the following statements. Put an "F" in the blank if the statement is a fact. Put an "O" in the blank if the statement is an opinion.

GENERAL ACTIVITY 8

_____ 1. Aunt Sponge and Aunt Spiker are mean to James.

_____ 2. In the story *Chocolate Fever*, Henry eats too much chocolate.

_____ 3. Maddie and Peggy are sorry they made fun of Wanda.

_____ 4. The boy takes apples from the giving tree.

_____ 5. Mafatu lacks courage.

_____ 6. Ramona is a pest.

_____ 7. Leslie Burke beats all the boys in the running race.

_____ 8. Pa Ingalls is a good hunter.

_____ 9. The secret garden is beautiful.

_____ 10. Colin is Mary's cousin.

_____ 11. Wilbur is a special pig.

_____ 12. Henry likes chocolate.

_____ 13. The reluctant dragon is ugly.

_____ 14. Sarah is lonesome for her home in Maine.

_____ 15. Fern takes care of Wilbur.

_____ 16. Everyone should have a Terabithia where they can go.

_____ 17. The giving tree likes giving its apples and branches to the boy.

_____ 18. Jemmy is whipped for things Prince Brat does.

_____ 19. Wanda likes the blue dress she wears to school everyday.

_____ 20. Sounder is a smart dog.

Directions
Specific literary elements (characterization, plot, theme, setting, point of view) are used to develop a story. The way these elements are developed make the difference between a good piece of literature and a bad piece of literature. The following explanations of literary elements can help you evaluate the books you read.

GENERAL ACTIVITY 9

Characterization: The way characters are developed. Characters are revealed through conversation, actions, and behaviors; through narration; and through comments of others.
Plot: The story line, the happenings that keep the reader involved and interested in the book.
Theme: The message or feeling that the author is trying to convey.
Setting: The where and the when of the story. The setting transports the reader to the time and the place of the story.
Point of View: The person through whose eyes the story unfolds. The story may be told in first person (I) or in third person (he/she/they).

Using the following grading scale, grade each literary element for a book you have read. Provide comments on why you assigned the grades you did.

Grading Scale
A = excellent
B = good
C = fair
D = not very good
F = not good

Title of book: _____

Author: _____

Grade	**Literary Element**	**Comments**
_____	Characterization	_____
_____	Plot	_____
_____	Theme	_____
_____	Setting	_____
_____	Point of view	_____

From *Read It Again: Book 2, A Guide for Teaching Reading Through Literature* published by Scott, Foresman and Company. Copyright © 1990 Liz Rothlein and Terri Christman.

Name _____ Date _____

Directions

In libraries, books are categorized by genres, which have certain characteristics. Some common genres are picture books, realistic fiction, historical fiction, fantasy, folktales, poetry, informational books, and biographies. Often it is easy to figure out which genre a book belongs to; yet many books overlap genres. Using the brief descriptions of genres provided, categorize each of the books you have read. Note: For more detailed information on genres, refer to *Children and Books*, by Zena Sutherland and May Hill Arbuthnot, and *Children's Literature in the Elementary School*, by Charlotte S. Huck, Susan Hepler, and Janet Hickman.

GENERAL ACTIVITY 10

Genre Descriptions

Realistic fiction: Fictitious but set in a plausible place and time. Realistic fiction often focuses on everyday problems, such as family issues, interpersonal problems, handicaps, sexism, aging, and death.

Historical fiction: Realistic and set in the past. One type of historical fiction is written in the past and uses fictional characters—there are no real people or recorded historical events—and yet the reader gets a feeling for the period in which the book was written. Another type of historical fiction involves actual people and recorded events.

Fantasy: Stories of enchantment, humorous tales, stories in which animals and toys are personified, and tales of science fiction. Fantasy books blend things that really couldn't happen in real life with realistic detail. Good fantasy involves at least one element of the possible within a framework of reality.

Books to Classify by Genre

Little House in the Big Woods	*Chocolate Fever*
Sounder	*Sarah, Plain and Tall*
Call It Courage	*Bridge to Terabithia*
Ramona the Pest	*The Secret Garden*
Charlotte's Web	*James and the Giant Peach*
The Lion, the Witch, and the Wardrobe	*The Giving Tree*
The Reluctant Dragon	*The Hundred Dresses*
The Whipping Boy	

Realistic Fiction

Historical Fiction

Fantasy

Name _____ Date _____

BOOK REPORT 1

Directions

Using a large sheet of paper (18 × 24), make a poster about one of your favorite books. Be creative so it will capture attention and make others want to read the book. Be sure to include the name of the book and the author. You might also include an illustration. Display the poster when it is completed. Note: Plan your poster by making a sketch of it in the space.

BOOK REPORT 2

Directions
Write a telegram, in 25 words or less, describing a favorite character in a book you have read.

Western Union

From *Read It Again: Book 2, A Guide for Teaching Reading Through Literature* published by Scott, Foresman and Company. Copyright © 1990 Liz Rothlein and Terri Christman.

**BOOK
REPORT 3**

Directions
Make a report of a book you have read by filling in the blanks.

Title of book: _____

_____

Author: _____

Illustrator: _____

Publisher: _____

_____

Copyright date: _____

Illustrate and write about the character you would most like to have as a friend. Explain your choice.

Illustrate and write about your favorite part of the book.

After completing the inside of the book, cut out the book and then fold on the dotted line and draw a new cover for the book.

BOOK REPORT 4

Directions

Book reviews are written and published in a variety of journals and magazines to help other people decide if they would like to read the book or not. Write a book review of your favorite book and compile it with other reviews written by your classmates. Include the following:

1. Bibliographical information: author, title, publisher, and publication date.
2. A brief summary of the story
3. A description of the main character(s)
4. The problem or conflict described in the story
5. A clue as to how the problem was solved
6. Your opinion of the book and your reason for that opinion

Also include a creative headline, an illustration, and a caption to go with the illustration.

Review:_____

_____

_____

_____

_____

_____

_____

_____

Illustration:

Caption:_____

From *Read It Again: Book 2, A Guide for Teaching Reading Through Literature* published by Scott, Foresman and Company. Copyright © 1990 Liz Rothlein and Terri Christman.

MAKING A BOOK

Materials

Lightweight cotton fabric
Scissors
Dry-mount tissue (from a photography shop or bookstore)
Cardboard (medium weight—needs to be heavier for larger books)
Iron or dry-mount press and tacking iron
Lightweight white paper for the pages of the book
Construction paper (color that contrasts or harmonizes with the cloth)
Needle and thread or long-arm stapler
Paste or glue

Directions

1. Cut the cloth to the size you need to cover the two sides of the book, with an inch overlap on all four edges of the cloth.
2. Cut the dry-mount tissue the same size as the cloth.
3. Cut the cardboard about an inch all the way around smaller than the dry-mount tissue and cloth.
4. Cut this piece of cardboard in half.
5. Place the dry-mount tissue evenly on top of the cloth.
6. Place the two pieces of cardboard on top of the dry-mount tissue. Leave about a half inch between the cardboard pieces and place them so there is an equal amount of dry-mount tissue and cloth on all sides.
7. Fold the cloth and dry-mount tissue at the corners, and with a hot iron press them to the cardboard. The heat of the iron makes the dry-mount tissue stick to both the cloth and the cardboard.
8. After all four corners are folded and ironed down, iron the side edges flat.
9. Fold the book cover and iron the front and back to make the cloth and cardboard stick together more securely.
10. Make a pattern for the pages by cutting a piece of paper a quarter inch less in length and width than the finished cover.
11. From the construction paper, cut an end page that is a little longer and wider than the book pages but that fits inside the cover.
12. Fold the book pages and the end page in the center. Sew or staple these pages together on the fold line.
13. Spread paste or glue over the back of the end paper. Adhere the pages to the book cover. Keep the book open and flat until the glue or paste is dry.

VOCABULARY WORDS

The following words are introduced and reinforced throughout this book.

absence
acquaintance
alone
ancient
appalling

betray
bloodthirsty
bluffing
branches
breeds
brindle
brougham

cabin
cargo
carried
castle
cautiously
chants
cholera
chore
climbed
closet
collapse
consolation
contentment
contest
contradicted
contrary
crown
cruel
curlicues

deference
desolate
despairing
detested
dignity
disagreeable
drawings
dreadful
dresses
dumbfounded
dusk

earnestly
eerie
enthralled
enticingly
eternal
exertions

familiar
famished
feelings
ferocious
foothills
forest
friendship

gape
gather
gloated
guard

hailstones
harbouring
haunches
hearth
hideous
hijacked
hoax
hollow
horrid
hundred

impaled
impending
imprisoned
imprudent
indifference
indignant
infuriated
inquisitive
intersection
irresolute
insidiously

jewels

kernels
kerosene

lantern
laughing
leaves
liberated
loathsome
logic
luminous
lurch

malevolently
mammoth
mercilessly
mirth
moor
murmur

nauseating
nuisance

obstinate
ominously

pandemonium
passage
phenomenon
plateau
popular
possum
preacher
predator
predicament
premises
premonition
prince
prodded
pungent

quarry

radiant
ravines
realm

reign
reproachfully
roamed
runt

saddle
sailed
scampered
school
scrawny
sewers
shade
sharecropper
shoaled
soldiers
solemn
speculation
spiteful
sporadically
squalls
straw tick
stern
stump
subservient
subsided
sulking
survive
swagger

teacher
terrific
thrashing
throne
traitor
trifle
trough
trundle bed
trunk

villains

waited
whickering
whip
wretched

From *Read It Again: Book 2, A Guide for Teaching Reading Through Literature* published by Scott, Foresman and Company. Copyright © 1990 Liz Rothlein and Terri Christman.

ANSWER KEY

Chocolate Fever

ACTIVITY 2

It happens at home.

a	n
m	

It happens at school.

b	g
c	h

It happens at the hospital.

d	j
i	

It happens while Henry is running away.

e	l
f	o
k	

ACTIVITY 3

1. b	5. h	9. c
2. d	6. k	10. e
3. i	7. f	11. j
4. g	8. a	12. l

Bridge to Terabithia

ACTIVITY 3
1. free
2. intermittently
3. indebted
4. kingdom
5. comfort
6. dangerously
7. thin
8. honor
9. unified

Charlotte's Web

ACTIVITY 1

1. F	5. O
2. O	6. O
3. O	7. O
4. F	8. F

ACTIVITY 3

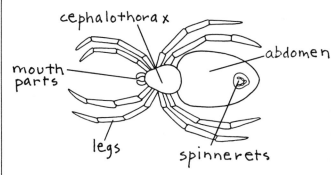

James and the Giant Peach

ACTIVITY 1

2	1
5	4
3	

Ramona the Pest

ACTIVITY 1

	1	2	3	4	5	6	7	8	9
True	M	(R)	(U)	T	(N)	(G)	J	A	(Y)
False	(E)	P	O	(H)	Y	L	(I)	(S)	W

H E N R Y   H U G G I N S
4 1 5 2 9   4 3 6 6 7 5 8

Call It Courage

ACTIVITY 1

From *Read It Again: Book 2, A Guide for Teaching Reading Through Literature* published by Scott, Foresman and Company. Copyright © 1990 Liz Rothlein and Terri Christman.

The Lion, the Witch, and the Wardrobe

ACTIVITY 2

a. fantasy
b. fantasy
c. reality
d. fantasy
e. reality

f. fantasy
g. fantasy
h. fantasy
i. reality
j. reality

1. i
2. c
3. d
4. f
5. j

6. e
7. a
8. b
9. g
10. h

Little House in the Big Woods

ACTIVITY 1

1. d
2. i
3. f
4. l
5. n

6. j
7. c
8. a
9. e
10. g

11. b
12. k
13. m
14. h
15. o

General Activity 1

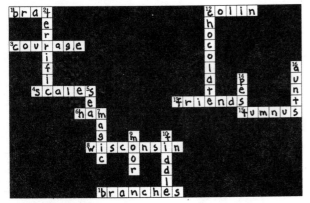

General Activity 3

Chocolate Fever	i
The Whipping Boy	f
The Hundred Dresses	g
The Secret Garden	e
Charlotte's Web	h
Call It Courage	b
Little House in the Big Woods	c
Sarah, Plain and Tall	a
Bridge to Terabithia	d

General Activity 8

1. F
2. O
3. O
4. F
5. O
6. O
7. F
8. O
9. O
10. F

11. O
12. F
13. O
14. O
15. F
16. O
17. O
18. F
19. O
20. O

General Activity 10*

REALISTIC FICTION
Bridge to Terabithia
Call It Courage
Chocolate Fever
The Hundred Dresses
Ramona the Pest

HISTORICAL FICTION
Little House in the Big Woods
Sarah, Plain and Tall
Sounder

FANTASY
Charlotte's Web
The Giving Tree
James and the Giant Peach
The Lion, the Witch, and the Wardrobe
The Reluctant Dragon
The Secret Garden
The Whipping Boy

*The books may fit into other genres as well.

From *Read It Again: Book 2, A Guide for Teaching Reading Through Literature* published by Scott, Foresman and Company. Copyright © 1990 Liz Rothlein and Terri Christman.